# DETOURS TO DESTINY

## When The Detour Becomes The Path

Keanna Lynette

Detours to Destiny: When The Detour Becomes The Path
Copyright © 2012 by Keanna Lynette Ralph
Published by Firestarters, LLC

ISBN 978-0692966389

Published by
Firestarters, LLC
970 Haddon Ave. #8743
Collingswood, NJ 08108

Revised Edition

Visit our Website at www.Firestartersmovement.com

Printed in the United States of America

2

# Acknowledgements

First, I have to thank my Lord and Savior Jesus Christ for giving me this book concept and also the courage to go through with it. I am eternally grateful that He saw something in me even when I couldn't see it in myself.

Next, I would like to thank my Spiritual Parents, Bishop John and Pastor Isha Edmondson for their love, support and wisdom over the years. I would like to thank Elder Yolonda Jones for playing a key role in my salvation experience and for inviting me out to a church that would one-day help change my life.

I would like to thank my family and friends for your love and support. Mom, thank you for showing me what it means to rise above your circumstances. Even as a single parent you instilled values in me that created stability and a desire to want more out of life. Special thanks to my second family—the Gnurdz. You are all a unique and awesome group of individuals and I would be remised if I didn't take the time to let you know how much I greatly appreciate each and every one of you!

Many thanks to my Aunt Renee and Uncle Bobby who took me in during my adolescent years and to my Aunt Pat who instilled in me a heart and desire for the things of God. It truly does take a village!

To Min. Kelley Sawyer, thank you for the part that you played in encouraging me to first begin this journey five years ago with the release of the first edition. I shall always remember and be grateful for that divine moment of destiny…God bless.

# Table of Contents

Foreword ........................................ 5

Preface ......................................... 7

Introduction .................................... 9

Detours, Detours, Detours ........................ 17

Where Are You ................................... 27

Deception, Excuses, Pride ....................... 35

The Great Fall .................................. 51

Strategic Positioning ........................... 65

The Pitfall of Rejection ........................ 73

The Dreaded D Word: Distractions ................ 83

Overextending Oneself ........................... 89

Relationship Detours ............................ 99

Not All Detours ................................. 109

Paradigm Shift .................................. 119

The Detour Is the Path .......................... 127

# Foreword

As Keanna's Pastors we are so proud of her growth and development in becoming an upcoming voice in her generation of hope, faith and achieving the impossible.

What you're about to read is not intended to be simply a good book, but rather a constant reminder of God's faithfulness in your life. In Detours to Destiny, Keanna sheds light on how regardless of what you are facing, you can overcome it and step into your destiny if you will just simply keep moving. As you read through the pages of this amazing tool for your life, you will be reminded that the same God who brought heroes of the faith through detours they faced to accomplish their destiny still desires to do the same through us today. The words on these pages will begin to change you from the inside out as Keanna speaks to the hiding places of insecurity and fear that have developed in your life from experiencing your own detours. She goes after activating your faith to inspire you to believe past the detour(s) you have experienced and makes a demand on the potential and destiny that may have been lying dormant inside you for years. By activating your faith to reconnect you with your God-sized potential, you will be inspired to live a life full of purpose.

We don't know anyone better positioned than Keanna to challenge you to rise above the mundane living and embrace your dream(s) again. Keanna, in sharing her own personal journey and experience of watching God move in spite of incredible detours, will push you and coach you out of accepting and conceding to the detour(s) in your life, into the realm of supernatural expectation. This book will show you that your hopes, dreams and expectations are truly just the beginning of what God can do.

Keanna's skillful combination of passion and practicality will both move you to want to live at a higher level of faith to achieve your destiny and equip you to get there. Detours to Destiny invokes the reader to embrace God's will for their life by strengthening their faith to believe in the impossible as you learn to live a life of boldness for the Kingdom of God.

Detours to Destiny is a must read. This book will stir you, shake you, and ultimately inspire you. It's a wake-up call for this generation to be audacious, to not settle for life in a spot where you hit a detour, but rather believe God for the impossible.

We are so excited about this book and it getting into the hands of as many people as possible. There are so many whom have stalled out in a place of life where they hit a detour. This book is going to serve as a jump start for your life to get you moving again with a new zeal, tenacity, and focus. It will cause you to refuse to be refused and deny to be denied by any past detour, as well as, future detours and become the person of destiny you were created to be.

*Bishop John & Pastor Isha Edmondson*
Victory In Christ Christian Center

# Preface

In a recent article published by Foxnews.com, host/author John Stossel sought to provide an answer to the old age question, "what makes people happy?" The response to this was the following: "People fantasize about leisure and luxury, but the best data shows that such things don't create lasting happiness. What does make for happiness is obtaining work that allows you to move toward goals that you find meaningful. In other words, what's important is not just employment, but purposeful work." I believe that the key word here is *meaningful*. In order for something to be meaningful to someone, it almost always has to coincide with their skillsets, passion, talents, abilities, and ultimately purpose unique to them as an individual. In other words, things become meaningful for a person when they have a natural inclination towards it and/or are simply wired in that direction. Inevitably this leads to destiny.

To be destined for a thing means that you were created and designed for that specific purpose. Similar to when someone says that person was destined to be a star, it indicates that there are innate qualities within that person seen early on that's attributed to those who become stars. So, even though they may not have reached that particular plateau in their lives as of yet, it doesn't take away from the fact that the potential to be one still lies within them. Likewise, I believe there are many reading this book who have qualities within them to go on and accomplish great things. However, for one reason or another, you are choosing to sit on it, allowing it to lie dormant as life passes you by. Perhaps the issue is you have not fully been convinced that your life carries a greater purpose that you have yet to see.

In Ephesians 1:5-6 we discover that God has "predestined us for adoption as sons through Jesus Christ, according to the purpose of his will, to the praise of his glorious grace, with which he has blessed us in the beloved." Moreover, these verses reveal to us that not only did God create us with a specific purpose in mind but because we are also blessed in Him, we can be assured that He has provided everything we need to go after it. While I won't go so far as to say that destiny is something that occurs overnight, I do believe that it can be kick-started once a person gets revelation of the purpose God has for them and then starts going after it. From then on, the pursuit of destiny really becomes a life long journey. A journey with many ups and downs, but when you know you're walking in your purpose you soon reach a point where the downs don't seem to matter as much. Instead, what does matter is the fact that you are now embarking on the ride of your life. This ride can also come with many uncertainties, so you must do your best to keep your eyes first and foremost on the one who is guiding you and then on the signs, instructions, and direction He gives.

## *Psalm 121*

"I lift up my eyes to the hills-- where does my help come from? My help comes from the LORD, the Maker of heaven and earth. He will not let your foot slip-- he who watches over you will not slumber; indeed, he who watches over Israel will neither slumber nor sleep. The LORD watches over you—the LORD is your shade at your right hand; the sun will not harm you by day, nor the moon by night. The LORD will keep you from all harm-- he will watch over your life; the LORD will watch over your coming and going both now and forevermore."

# Introduction

*"Focus on the journey, not the destination. Joy is found not in finishing an activity but in doing it."*

–Greg Anderson

I'm not sure where you may be on your journey right now, but I know for me this particular journey began in the year 2005. I found myself in a very dark place, not knowing what to do concerning my life. My future was supposed to be sunny and bright, yet all I could see was dark clouds and gloom. On the surface, I was an ambitious young, motivated twenty-something year old who had just completed grad school but beneath it all I was broke, jobless, and practically homeless—having no true place to call home. After moving out of the college dorms, I ended up staying with my cousin for a few months, using half of my $200 unemployment check to contribute towards the rent. I also made it a point to try and help out in other ways by babysitting, cleaning, etc. Still, I continued to have that empty feeling of not being able to pull my own weight and it bothered me. You see, I had expected so much more out of life and truthfully, out of MYSELF. Not only did I begin to feel disappointed but I began to feel like a disappointment.

Eventually, I reached a breaking point. I cried out to God in desperate anguish complaining "this isn't how my life is supposed to be!" In fact, I believe I had this conversation with Him on a quite a number of occasions, but in this particular instance, I can remember laying prostrate across my cousin's living room floor absolutely exhausted and sleep deprived as we worked into the wee hours of the night getting the place ready for her quarterly inspection. Since I was the one without the job at the time, it was my responsibility to wait around for the inspector to come. So of course I took this as another opportunity to once again voice my frustrations. There I was pouring my heart and soul out to God. "Lord, I just don't understand…I thought you were going to look out for me…is this really my lot.…When will things change…I can't do this much longer." These were just some of the thoughts and questions that flowed out of my mind and off of my lips. Then, somewhere in the midst of all this, I felt God gently tug on my heart as He impressed on me the words: "Detours to Destiny." Detours to Destiny…what am I supposed to do with that, I wondered? God went on to share with me how everything in my life whether good or bad was ultimately being used for a purpose, including that which I was going through at that very moment. From this encounter, I also gained a whole new appreciation for Romans 8:28 which says, "And we know that in all things God works for the good of those who love him, who have been called according to his purpose."

I began to understand more that day how divinely orchestrated all of our ups, downs, and well…Detours are. At the end of the day, God is sovereign and there is nothing, absolutely nothing that can happen in our lives without Him first signing off on it. I had to accept that even the not so good things in my life were part of God's plan to work out something greater, something that I may not have fully seen or could comprehend at that time. Still, I had to be at peace in knowing that God had a plan and more than anything He was in control!

I also came to the realization that part of God's plan concerning my own trials and setbacks was attributed to His purpose for me to write this book. He encouraged me with the fact that one day people who didn't even know me would be inspired through the experiences and victories that would be retold in part through this book. As a result, the fact that I didn't quite understand everything didn't matter as much because what became more relevant were the lives that would be impacted simply by me sharing this story.

## The Birthing

Fast forward seven years--while I had never forgotten the day the Lord dropped "Detours to Destiny" in my heart, somehow life had a way of drowning it out. Once I began working full time, getting more involved in ministry and taking on the responsibility of helping to raise my nephew, it just appeared there was little room left to do anything else— including writing a book. Everything else became more important while thoughts of purpose and destiny drifted further and further away from my mind. Then all of that changed on June 2, 2012. While at an Empowerment Conference, I walked into a workshop entitled "Rejected, But I Still Made It." It was on this day that I realized I no longer had to be held captive to my past, but in fact could use it as a tool to catapult me into my destiny.

Prior to this workshop I had been praying for God's direction and even more specifically for a mentor, which as a side note can be crucial to one's overall development (Proverbs 11:14). Not only does having a mentor help you gain good godly counsel, but if you choose well, your mentor should also give you a glimpse of your own future/destiny. There should be something they are successfully doing in their own lives that you can see yourself doing in your own one day. This does not mean you will become a mirror image of them, but you should be able to learn something from them that will be instrumental to your own purpose. After listening to the speaker, I knew instantly that God had answered my prayer at that moment and that I was indeed sitting in front of my soon to be mentor for that season. The reason why I knew this to be true is I had peace about it. While I had been to numerous conferences and workshops, there was a point of connection formed with this one like no other. Yes, the message was great, but it didn't stop there. It left this unction inside me letting me know that there was more purpose in me sitting there that day and it went beyond the workshop itself. It was a divinely orchestrated moment that God used to connect me with the person who would be instrumental in helping me get to jumpstart my journey towards destiny.

So with half boldness and half nervousness I approached her after it was all over and introduced myself. I shared with her the fact that I had been praying for a mentor and that I believed God had led me to her and asked if she would be willing to take it on—all the while understanding that mentorship can never be taken as a light thing. As such I was pleasantly surprised and relieved that she humbly accepted. We exchanged some more words and then afterwards she gave me a big hug. I believe it was at this point that I then completely broke down. As the tears began streaming down my face, I felt as if a load was being taken off of me, as if walls were beginning to be torn down, as if I was beginning to be set free from something. To this day, I am still not completely sure what took place in those seconds but I do know that from that day forward my life instantly began to change.

The next day when I went to church, a sister who operates with the gift of wisdom, approached me and said "Keanna, I had a dream about you last night." She then proceeded to tell me that in this dream I had given birth to a beautiful baby boy. Of course, the first thing that popped up in my mind was "baby? I'm not married!" Then, as if on one accord we both realized that the Lord was trying to reveal something else—the dream was meant to be symbolic of something that the Lord intended to birth through me—something other than a child at that time. Immediately both of us got excited knowing that whenever God is trying to birth anything through us it can only be something good (even though sometimes the process leading up to it could bring forth some labor pains). I walked away from that conversation with a heart of expectation, believing that God had something great in store and that He would soon bring revelation to me of what that something great would be.

The very next night I then dreamed that I was in labor. It appeared that I was some place like my home and there was a doctor and nurse there trying to help deliver the baby. I kept hearing them say to me "keep pushing, keep pushing." They told me that they could feel the crown so I was almost there but I had to keep at it. At that point, I began to feel the pain more and more and attempted to stop and take a break. I imagine that at this time thoughts of perhaps stopping altogether may have entered my mind, yet I knew that I couldn't because the process had already begun. During this brief intermission, the doctor or nurse; can't remember which one it was exactly but they gave me a washcloth and began to wipe some of the sweat off my brow and encouraged me to keep going. What happened soon after I can't really say because I woke up not too long after this point, wondering if I had ever finished giving birth and even more, what God was truly saying to me. I remember eventually journaling about these two dreams and specifically asking God to give me clarity on them. Then as if on perfect key, not even an hour after I finished writing about it, He brought forth the revelation I was seeking.

Within that next hour I received a call from my mentor and she began to tell me how God had laid me on her heart regarding an upcoming Writer's Intensive that her Publishing company would soon be hosting. Although I did mention prior to this conversation that I hoped to write a book someday, I had made it clear that it was someday in the future and that I wasn't ready. So as she began to discuss more in detail how she felt strongly it was purposed for me to be there, I began to immediately doubt myself. I had every excuse in the book at that point and in my mind they were all valid. For one, I didn't have enough time to do all the other things I was already committed to do, how could I possibly take on another project. Two, I was still unemployed at the time and gearing up to start back with my doctoral studies, how could I take on another financial burden. Three, I was still growing in Christ with still so much more to go, how could anyone possibly find value in what I would have to say…and the list just went on and on. I was not ready for it, but then she took me by surprise.

As I began to give her some of the reasons why I wasn't ready to pursue the call to write, mainly stating the fact that I wasn't prepared perhaps the biggest factor of them all, she then insisted we do a quick exercise. "Ok," I thought, "I like exercises." Besides, I was already convinced by this point that there was almost nothing she could say that would change my mind (stubbornness at its best☺). Un-phased by my rigid stance she began to ask me a series of questions that went like this: "Keanna, do you have any children?" No, I responded. "Do you know anyone around you who does have children", she asked. "Yes, of course," I replied. "Do you think they were fully prepared for those children prior to having them," she added. "No, not really", I said. "Do you think that if you were pregnant, you would feel like you were ready to birth that child?" she went

14

on. (By this point my jaw was practically on the floor). "After reading all the baby books you could and preparing the best you can for that child, would you then feel like you were fully prepared to birth it?" "No," I replied trying to fight back the tears. By the end of the dialogue she helped me to see that similar to having a baby, you will often feel ill prepared in pursuing your calling and destiny but you can't allow this feeling of inadequacy to cause you to abort the dream. The fact of the matter is it has to be faith that propels you forward, faith in knowing that "the one who calls you is faithful and He will do it" (1 Thessalonians 5:24).

*It will be faith to propel you forward and faith that will keep you, so don't be afraid to stand on it.*

## Reflection Point

From then on I came to understand that many times there is indeed purpose in the detours that life may bring our way and even though it may bring pain with it at times, we still must keep believing, keep trusting and keep moving along knowing all the while that God is in control.

So this was the beginning of my new found journey. Again, I'm not sure where you are in your particular journey or whether you've even accepted the challenge to begin it in the first place but one thing I know to be sure, whatever journey you choose to begin with God, He will be faithful to see you through its completion. So be sure to stop and smell the roses now and then as you enjoy the process of stepping into your destiny.

# Detours, Detours, Detours

*"You're on the road to success when you realize that failure is only a detour."*

−Anonymous

According to the Merriam Dictionary, a detour can be defined as "a deviation from a direct course or the usual procedure; especially: a roundabout way temporarily replacing part of a route." In other words, detours can take us off what can be the most direct and shortest route and place us on an extended path that still gets us to our destination but, in many cases, in a longer amount of time and with much more scenery/coverage and experience. Perhaps, one of the most infamous detours is the one that the children of Israel took on their way to the Promised Land. What should have taken them less than 2 weeks to travel, ultimately took a total of 40 years to complete. Why, you may ask? The simple answer to this question is that there were lessons to be learned. Similar to what you'll often discover in your own detours in life. Many times, there are simply lessons to be learned.

When I consider the physical detour signs used for directing traffic, what I find to be most interesting about it is its distinct color and shape. It's bright orange color and diagonal rectangular shape makes it difficult to miss, and rightfully so since the consequences of overlooking one can result in an entire trip being thrown off. Additionally, its striking orange color can also serve as a warning sign that if not heeded to can pose problems or threats ahead. Still, what it may tend to indicate most of the time is that a work is in progress. In fact, under most traffic regulations, detour signs are typically categorized within the Work Zone Category. This simply means whenever road work is being performed on the highway, these signs are displayed to advise you and guide you through the work area. So ultimately they serve as a directional guide to help get you through possible bumps in the road as you make your way to your destination.

*Therefore, my dear friends, as you have always obeyed—not only in my presence, but now much more in my absence—continue to WORK OUT your salvation with fear and trembling,*
*-Philippians 2:12*

### I Saw the Sign

Sometime in the early nineties, a Swedish pop band called Ace of Base came out with a song entitled "The Sign." Though I may not agree with everything about this song, I must admit that the lyrics are quite catchy, particularly this following excerpt, which says:

*I saw the sign and it opened up my eyes, I saw the sign*
*Life is demanding without understanding*
*I saw the sign and it opened up my eyes, I saw the sign*
*No one's gonna drag you up to get into the light*
*where you belong*
*But where do you belong?*

So much can be taken out of these fives lines alone, but as to not get too far ahead of myself, for now I will simply focus on the first three lines. Here, the emphasis is on first simply being able to see the sign and then two, drawing the necessary and intended meaning out of it in order to experience change. Ultimately this should result in what we would describe in a later chapter as an "Aha!" moment. In today's society where we're constantly inundated with countless banners, billboards, and other forms of advertisement it can often become challenging enough just to get to the first step of seeing a particular sign let alone drawing meaning from it. However, I believe that when necessary God will go to great lengths to help make the signs in our lives crystal clear so that we are able to see His intended direction and purpose for our lives. Our job is to simply not avoid them.

## Don't Bypass the Signs in Your Life

Some months back I had decided that it was time to return back to my doctoral studies since I had finally finished the two certificate programs I signed up to complete at my previous university. I was stuck on the fact that this was my time to go ahead and get it all done in one shot while there were still months remaining to collect my unemployment benefits. It was around this time that I also made the decision to embark on this new-found journey to publish this book. Then out of nowhere as if it was all scripted out, I received notification from the State of NJ informing me that they had now suspended the extended unemployment benefits and instead of it continuing into the following year like it was supposed to, I would now be receiving my very last check that following month. SHOCKED and BAFFLED are the first two words that come to mind to describe how I felt at that moment. I mean, I had specifically planned out the whole next 6 months or so believing that I was going to still be covered but now that was no longer the case.

After a few moments I was able to finally calm down and ultimately put the whole situation in God's hands trusting Him for the outcome. Then, I concluded that what was happening was nothing but the enemy trying to get me to back down from doing what I was supposed to be doing at that time concerning school and this book. While this turned out to be true in one respect, I would soon find it wasn't in another.

Not long after receiving my last unemployment check in July I ended up having a very candid conversation with my good friend Timothy one evening. I was telling him how excited I was to be starting back up with my doctoral studies that following week and how determined I was to not let all of these other things going on in my life hinder or distract me. In other words, I was focused and had decided that come hell or high water I was moving forward. Moreover, I felt like I was prepared for just about anything—that was anything except for what followed next in this particular dialogue. It went something like this:

Me: I'm so excited about finally moving forward with my studies now! I think the enemy may have been trying to get me off focus with it, but I'm determined to work my way through it.

Timothy: What exactly do you mean, Keanna?

Me: Well, it's just a lot of stuff going on in my life right now that I don't seem to understand. Certain doors that used to be open are all of sudden now closing on me. For instance, unemployment was supposed to remain in effect until I finished my schooling but out of nowhere this has all changed.

Timothy: Oh wow…really?

Me: Yeah but I'm trying to not concern myself with all of that. Right now I just need to focus on maintaining some kind of balance because I have a lot of other things going on between ministry, reactivating my business, building a new job support group, finishing this book and now of course getting ready for school to start next week. I don't want to get overwhelmed by all of this.

Timothy: Yeah, I feel you. That is a lot. Now, explain to me again why you're starting back up with school again in the midst of all of this.

Me: Well, pursuing a doctorate degree is something I always wanted to do and this seems like the best time to do it while I'm not currently working.

Timothy: Oh, I see….and what did God say?

Me: (Brief uncomfortable pause) Umm…well, I do believe that this is something that He would want me to do. I feel like it definitely lines up with what He's doing in my life.

Timothy: I can believe that…but is He telling you to do it right now? It kind of sounds like to me that you haven't completely put it before Him.

Me: I mean, I did initially but not necessarily recently. Besides, like I said this seems like the perfect time except for all the crazy things going on in my life right now.

Timothy: Hmm… Keanna, I'm not so sure if I would consider all of that as crazy. However, what I do think can be crazy is seeing a person driving down a road and see caution sign after caution sign indicating that there is a cliff up ahead but fail to take heed to any of those precautions and still end up falling off of the very cliff that could have been avoided. Now that would be crazy.

Me: Long pause…(crickets chirping…followed by long sigh)…Ok…fine I will be open to what the Lord may want to say to me concerning this situation. Still, this doesn't mean that I'm pulling out of the program. I'm just willing to be more open to any signs the Lord may be trying to give me.

Timothy: Amen, and I pray that He does just that!

I hung up that evening having a sincere heart in wanting to know what the Lord wanted me to do concerning the school situation and as fate we have it, it didn't take long for Him to make His will crystal clear. That next morning I woke up about 7am in order to take a trip down to Social Services. Now that my unemployment had officially run out and so had my savings, I felt as if there was no other choice but to now apply for Public Assistance. When I got there the place was relatively packed but to my surprise they were still able to take me and even to my greater surprise it didn't take long at all. By the time 10am rolled around I was in the back with the counselor going through the application process. Towards the end of the interview, in one of the final questions she asked if I was currently enrolled in school. Proudly I said, "Well yes I am but I don't officially start till Monday." That's when she broke the news to me and said "Oh, I see…in that case you wouldn't be eligible for any financial assistance." "Excuse me", I responded. I thought being in school is a good thing. "Well, it is" she said but the only way you would still qualify while in school is if you were disabled, worked a part-time job of 20 hours or more, was in a work study program, or had a child that was 12 years or younger and since none of this applies to you then you would not be eligible." "Ok, let me get this straight," I replied. "You mean to tell me that someone who has a clear drug or alcohol habit can come up here and apply and have no problem qualifying for benefits, but for me because I'm in school I'm not eligible?" "Yes, pretty much…I don't make the rules, I just follow them," she added. "Wow," was all I could bring myself to say in response to that. Even further, I was thinking to myself, well God you do work fast. You see, it was at this point it all became crystal clear. I contacted my friend later that day to inform Him that God had spoken and although crushed in the process, I had made the decision to obey. In effect, I had seen the sign. I didn't necessarily like it, but I accepted it nonetheless.

Now, looking back I understand more and more why God allowed this to be. There was just no way I would have been able to focus on my studies while also accomplishing everything else on my plate, particularly this book. From this experience I learned how important it is to take heed to God's directional signs even if it seems to be taking us off the path we're supposed to be on. You never know how bumps or pitfalls lying on the road to success will cause you to be redirected to another route in order to avoid something and then bring you back on your path once you have passed them by. Truly, His ways are perfect and His signs are heaven sent.

*"As for God, his way is perfect; the word of the LORD is flawless. He is a shield for all who take refuge in him." –II Samuel 22:31*

On a more serious note, I can also recall a time when taking heed to one of God's signs nearly saved my life. This particular situation took place some years back when I was in college. I had just experienced a bad falling out with a close friend of mine, and was feeling really bad about the part I had played. Ultimately, I knew I allowed my emotions to get the best of me that night and realized I said things that I shouldn't have. Once it was all over and I began to make my way back home to Jersey, thoughts continued to flow through my head and intensify. I went from wishing things had went differently to literally beating myself up about the whole ordeal. In hindsight I realize now that it was simply an attack from the enemy, especially seeing how things rapidly took a turn for the worse.

As I began to approach the Ben Franklin Bridge, the thoughts in my mind suddenly escalated to suicidal ones where I started thinking that it would just be best to kill myself and get over all my problems and issues. I figured this way I wouldn't have to worry about missing the mark or doing something in life I would later regret. I was beating myself up pretty bad. Eventually, thoughts of running my car off the Ben Franklin

Bridge began to consume me and I became convinced that this was what I should go ahead and do. I proceeded to map it all out, playing it out in my mind play by play how I was going to get over the rails to be successful. In my mind I was all ready to go, the only thing I needed to do first was get past the final stoplight before the bridge and then it was smooth sailing from there. As I approached this final red light I took notice of a homeless man standing outside holding up a sign asking for food. Although it's not uncommon to see homeless people in this area during the day, I found it unusual he was out there so late in the evening that night. Nonetheless, I figured it was nice to be able to carry out one final good deed before taking that plunge. So I stopped where he was and went to hand him some money. What happened after this not only surprised me, but also helped spare my life that evening! After I gave him the money, he said thank you but then looked me straight in the eye as if he knew what I was contemplating and with all sincerity said, "Drive Safely." Drive safely? I thought to myself. "When was the last time someone on the streets said that to me?" I pondered. Then, realized such had never occurred till that very moment. Immediately realizing how much of a divine appointment that was, I knew that this man, or perhaps angel, was a divine sign from God to stop me from heading towards a certain direction and thankfully I got the message!

I ended up driving the rest of my way home that night in tears as I pondered on the Father's love and mercy towards me. While I had it in my heart to carry out something really stupid based off of my emotions, God in His divine orchestration blocked it! The awesome part is that He didn't do it by forcing His will on me, but He did it through sending me a sign. Just as a loving Father would He sent me an unlikely message that was used to get my attention and stop me from going in my own selfish way. Moreover, I believe that God does this with all of His children. He sends us all signs used as warnings to help us avert possible danger. 1 Corinthians 10:13 makes it clear that "No temptation has seized you except what is common to man. And God is faithful; he will not let you be tempted beyond what you can bear. But when you are tempted, he will also provide a way out so that you can stand up under it." Regardless of what our situation may be God will never leave us totally hanging where we are left to make the tough decisions, especially the life threatening ones, on our own. Rather He will always provide a way of escape. The key is we must be willing to hearken unto His call.

## Reflection Point

Is it possible that God may be trying to send you messages concerning your own direction in life? Have you turned off the transmitter or are you an open vessel willing to hear whatever it is He may have to say concerning your situation? Determining this may make the difference between your next breakthrough or breakdown.

Whatever you do, I pray that you make the decision today to not avoid the signs. It can be detrimental to your destiny.

# Where Are You?

*"Don't let life discourage you; everyone who got where he is had to begin where he was."*

-Richard L. Evans

Before moving forward, let me share a little excerpt from my journal that will help shed clarity on how this chapter even came about:

June 6, 2012

I felt like the day started off good but by the time the evening rolled around I seemingly lost my wind. The next thing I knew it was 11pm and I was watching the movie Bridesmaids while eating an ice cream bar and a packet of butterscotch Krimpets. It was a good movie; however, I was saddened to find such parallelism in the main character's life to mine. Although I wasn't having sex with a man who considered me option #3 on his list, I still somehow felt that I settled for so many years in the relationship area. I'm not sure why it's so easy for us to cling on to something for so long even when we see clearly it's not going anywhere. Anyway, I digress. So here I am 11 o'clock at night drowning my sorrows in fatty foods all the while losing the last bit of motivation I had to tackle the remainder of my goals. It was truly pitiful but nonetheless, I had to recognize where I was. I was at a place in my life where I felt as if I had hit rock bottom. In addition to having just ended a dead end, off and on again, 7-year relationship, I also found myself unemployed, in debt from student loans, and ultimately unfulfilled in life. Nevertheless, the silver lining in all of this is that it ultimately helped me to discover another chapter for this book, Where Are You? This stems from the passage in Genesis where God asks Adam this same question. Well, I feel like I finally discovered where I am and I don't particularly like it so it's now time to move on!

There is a quote by a man named Carl Jung that says: "Your vision will become clear only when you can look into your own heart. Who looks outside, dreams; who looks inside, awakes." That particular day or rather for this particular season of my life, I had to take a deep look into my own heart knowing that many times what we see on the surface level is only a manifestation of what exists within. As such it was time to begin pulling away the layers, to discover those deep things hidden within. And similar to King David in Psalm 139:23 I too had to cry out and say "Search me, O God, and know my heart; test me and know my anxious thoughts (NIV)." For only He truly knows the deepest depths of our hearts, and the things that are often hidden from even our own selves. Here, I am reminded of the dialogue that took place in John 21 between Jesus and Peter which went like this (NIV):

When they had finished eating, Jesus said to Simon Peter, "Simon son of John, do you love me more than these?"

"Yes, Lord," he said, "you know that I love you."

Jesus said, "Feed my lambs."

Again Jesus said, "Simon son of John, do you love me?"

He answered, "Yes, Lord, you know that I love you."

Jesus said, "Take care of my sheep."

The third time he said to him, "Simon son of John, do you love me?"

Peter was hurt because Jesus asked him the third time, "Do you love me?" He said, "Lord, you know all things; you know that I love you."

I believe that part of the reason why Jesus asked Peter this question several times is because he wanted Peter to really search his own heart, and not just give a quick surface response. How many times have you been asked a question and without much thought quickly blurted out a reply. I know that I've been guilty of it on numerous occasions. The fact of the matter is that when Peter said to Jesus "Lord you know all things" he was completely accurate. God does know everything about us, and it's His goal that we too understand as much about us as we possibly can for as Aristotle would put it "knowing thyself is the beginning of wisdom". Still, we must understand that achieving this can never be done apart from God because in Him lies ALL WISDOM.

I have often heard Bishop John Edmondson say, whenever you want to know the purpose of a thing, you never ask the thing itself but you ask the maker of the thing. This means you don't ask the vacuum cleaner how to use it, but you refer to the manual that was created by the manufacturer. Our manual is the Bible and God, the manufacturer created it purposely so we didn't have to stumble through life constantly wondering who we are and what it is we were purposed to accomplish. He doesn't want to trick us or keep us in the dark concerning His will but rather He has every intention on revealing His purposes and plans for our lives. We just have to be willing to search it out. Matthew

7:7 says: "Ask and it will be given to you; seek and you will find; knock and the door will be opened to you." Sometimes, we just aren't willing to take the steps necessary to get to this place. Laziness can cause us to expect things to just drop in our laps waiting for God to miraculously change our situations when God is waiting on us to become the change! In the words of Theodore Roosevelt, "Do what you can, with what you have, where you are."

Still, it is important that while you are moving forward in this process that you aren't embarking on it alone, but rather learning to depend on God to reveal all of the things that you need to know about yourself and your present situation.

*"For he will bring our darkest secrets to light and will reveal our private motives…"- 1 Corinthians 4:5*

Remember that God wants you to win. He is on your side and thus will always work to give you what you need to be successful, including the revelation of knowing *where you are*. Your part is to listen, accept, and move forward. This is why I believe there is so much truth in the statement: to know where you are going in life, you must first know and accept where you currently are. Just knowing isn't enough; it's a start but acceptance must follow if true change is to occur. Moreover, please understand that accepting where you are doesn't mean you have to be okay with it and think that it's just the way things have to be and remain. However, it does mean that you should recognize the fact that you are where you are for a reason and then make the changes necessary to move forward. The good news is that as in the words of G.I. Joe, "Knowing is half the battle," so once you get to this place you're already half way there!

# Press Pass the Norm

*"It helps, I think, to consider ourselves on a very long
journey: the main thing is to keep to the faith, to endure, to help
each other when we stumble or tire, to weep and press on."*
—Mary Richards

Getting through the next half of the journey will be predicated mostly on your ability and willingness to press through and press on. Like any other journey in life, there will always be bumps and challenges on the road ahead, but ultimately, it will be our persistence and stick-to-itiveness which will determine whether or not we obtain the expected end and promises of God. In fact, Hebrews 10:36 offers this insight, "For you have need of endurance, so that when you have done the will of God you may receive what is promised." You have to learn to look at your journey towards destiny as a marathon and not as a sprint; as such endurance is extremely crucial.

Endurance will allow you to keep pressing on when you have surpassed the normal threshold of pain and strength. Anyone who has ever worked out knows what I'm talking about. When you are really serious about creating lasting results through your work out, you make it a point to press beyond the normal threshold of pain. I can recall this happening to me some months back after returning back to the gym after a long sabbatical. For the first couple of days I took it fairly easy but then something in me said, go deeper, press harder. So I decided to work out to the point where I would normally get tired and end it out but this time kept going and pushed harder. While my body began to throb and ache and sweat dripped down profusely, I pressed forward with a made up mind that I wasn't going to back down until I reached a new threshold no matter how painful it was. In order to do this I had to take my focus off of the pain and redirect it towards God and towards my ultimate goal. I told myself that it was mind over matter and that as long as my mind was focused on this, then the pain wouldn't matter. Yes, it was complete agony but eventually I became numb to it because the eye of the tiger was in full effect and not even the pain was going to stop me from moving forward.

I believe we need to take this same tenacity and apply it towards our pursuit towards destiny. Regardless, of the pain we feel and the emotions we have to endure, there has to be a made up mind that come hell or high water, we're pressing through. There has to be a resolve within that our response to the detours and challenges will remain consistent at all times despite what situations and circumstances look like. Moreover, it's a necessity that we see our current adversities as only a stepping stone to our destiny. In a book entitled "It's Not Over" by Ricardo Sanchez, he discusses the important point of how to keep going even when you feel like you're losing the fight:

"There is a graduation that occurs at the end of struggle that can catapult you into your next season, if you allow it and surrender to it. The journey of struggle involves release. You must fling yourself into the arms of Jesus and trust He is at work in your situation…When you release yourself to the process of struggle, you learn to fight. You develop muscle endurance and strength and gain a confidence in your mission and purpose."

A common thread throughout this book is that there are certain qualities built within us during the greatest struggles in life, so it is important to not cast them off as just another thing you have to deal with but instead look at these challenges as something that can help drive you closer to your destiny. View it as another opportunity to grow the wings you need to really soar and fly into your ultimate purpose in life. I believe Romans 5:3-4 states it best:, "More than that, we rejoice in our sufferings, knowing that suffering produces endurance, and endurance produces character, and character produces hope…(ESV)." Again, one of the key words here is endurance. You must be willing to endure and press on. Don't give up; don't throw in the towel but when the going gets tough, show your adversities that you are a force to be reckoned with.

In closing, I am reminded of a famous poem written by well-known poet, Edgar A. Guest entitled "Don't Quit" that I believe speaks to the heart of this matter.

### Don't Quit

When things go wrong, as they sometimes will,
When the road you're trudging seems all up hill,
When the funds are low, and the debts are high,
And you want to smile, but you have to sigh,
When care is pressing you down a bit,
Rest if you must, but don't you quit.

Life is queer with its twists and turns,
As every one of us sometimes learns,
And many a failure turns about,
When he might have won had he stuck it out.
Don't give up though the pace seems slow,
You may succeed with another blow.

Success is failure turned inside out,
The silver tint of the clouds of doubt,
And you never can tell how close you are,
It may be near when it seems so far,
So stick to the fight when you're hardest hit,

It's when things seem worse,
That you must not quit.

## Reflection Point

I think it's safe to say that everyone has struggled with thoughts of giving up at some point or even numerous points in their lives, but fortunately thinking it and doing it are two totally different things. Nonetheless, they can be very closely aligned. Proverbs 23:7 tells us that "as a man thinketh in his heart so he is." Author James Allen in his book, "As a Man Thinketh" takes it a step further by stating, "A man is literally what he thinks, his character being the complete sum of all his thoughts."

From this we are able to see how vital thoughts are in dictating one's actions. Therefore, it's imperative that as you move forward, you do so taking on the right thoughts to keep you on your journey. Make it a point every day to mediate on at least one positive thought, scripture, quote, etc. that you can use as motivation to continue forward on your journey. You are free to pull out any of the ones that you have come across in this book or search out your own, but make it a priority to keep it at the center of your mind especially when battling with thoughts of giving up. Remember, where the mind goes, the feet are not far behind so keep your thoughts in line with the word of God.

*"Watch your thoughts, for they become words.*
*Watch your words, for they become actions.*
*Watch your actions, for they become habits.*
*Watch your habits, for they become character.*
*Watch your character, for it becomes your destiny"*
*-Unknown*

# Deception Excuses, Pride:
## Common Roadblocks to Destiny

Oftentimes, in order to get to the place of knowing, accepting, and then doing something about where you are, you must conquer a few common roadblocks along the way. The first roadblock can be the trickiest, and in fact, became the cause of the greatest fall known to man--Deception.

### Roadblock I: Deception

*"All deception in the course of life is indeed nothing else but a lie reduced to practice, and falsehood passing from words into things."-Robert Southey*

One of the greatest and most costly deceptions that ever took place in history occurred in the Garden of Eden between Eve and the serpent. Here is the account as described in Genesis 3:1-13 (NIV):

*1 Now the serpent was more crafty than any of the wild animals the Lord God had made. He said to the woman, "Did God really say, 'You must not eat from any tree in the garden'?"*
*2 The woman said to the serpent, "We may eat fruit from the trees in the garden, 3 but God did say, 'You must not eat fruit from the tree that is in the middle of the garden, and you must not touch it, or you will die.'"*

*4 "You will not certainly die," the serpent said to the woman. 5 "For God knows that when you eat from it your eyes will be opened, and you will be like God, knowing good and evil."*

*6 When the woman saw that the fruit of the tree was good for food and pleasing to the eye, and also desirable for gaining wisdom, she took some and ate it. She also gave some to her husband, who was with her, and he ate it. 7 Then the eyes of both of them were opened, and they realized they were naked; so they sewed fig leaves together and made coverings for themselves.*

*8 Then the man and his wife heard the sound of the Lord God as he was walking in the garden in the cool of the day, and they hid from the Lord God among the trees of the garden. 9 But the Lord God called to the man, "Where are you?"*

*10 He answered, "I heard you in the garden, and I was afraid because I was naked; so I hid." 11 And he said, "Who told you that you were naked? Have you eaten from the tree that I commanded you not to eat from?"*

*12 The man said, "The woman you put here with me—she gave me some fruit from the tree, and I ate it." 13 Then the Lord God said to the woman, "What is this you have done?"*

*The woman said, "The serpent deceived me, and I ate."*

Just as Satan used a question to cast doubt in Eve's mind and eventually cause her to sin against God, so he attempts to do the same thing with us. One moment, we can be completely certain and confident in the dreams God gave us, then a question arises out of nowhere that immediately causes doubt and gets us to walk away from our passion. We begin to question God, question if we heard from Him correctly, or even question our capability to do what He said. The next thing we know, we've somehow counted ourselves out altogether or allowed someone else to. It's the old pull the wool over the eyes trick and the scariest part is that, many times, we don't even realize it's there.

## Don't Be Self-Deceived

Have you ever met a person who was so stuck in their own way that no matter how much you tried to convince them otherwise, it was simply pointless? For example, you can tell them that the sky is blue until you are blue in the face yourself but because they are so deceived into thinking its red; all you end up doing is wasting your breath. I imagine that this is what it may look like when we are walking in self-deception. We can reach a point where no matter how much God may try to tug on our hearts regarding a certain area, we continue in the direction in which we believe to be right in our own eyes. Similar to how in Genesis 3:6 when it says that Eve looked at the fruit and saw that it was pleasing to her eyes (NIV). This is typically the beginning place of self-deception—when we begin to esteem or place more weight on how we view a certain thing in our lives, whether it remains to be true or not or according to God's word or not. Moreover, like many other slippery slopes in our lives, we usually don't realize what's happening until we're quickly tumbling down.

It was not too long ago that I found myself to be right in this very place, and it first began a little over 7 years ago. I had reached a point in my life where I felt as if I was ripe for marriage and had inadvertently convinced myself that my time had come, and even more, that the person I was only meant to be friends with was my husband. This was the first mistake I made. You see, once you get to the point where your mind is made up about something you lose objectivity and then begin to force everything into place. It reminds me of a jigsaw puzzle...there have been times when I became so anxious to finish out the puzzle that I took pieces that I knew didn't belong but tried to force it to fit just so I could say the puzzle was complete.

So, here I was convinced that marriage had to be on the horizon for me. Although I was still fresh in my twenties it just seemed right for me to settle down early on. Besides part of my script (you know the line by line playwright of how we feel our lives are supposed to play out) included me being married with children by 25 so I felt there was little time to waste. Mistake two was I made it all about me. While it's nothing wrong with setting goals and dreams, the problem comes in when we neglect to submit them to God. Proverbs 19:21 tells us that "Many are the plans in a person's heart, but it is the Lord's purpose that prevails." We have to understand that at the end of the day, God always has the final say on what comes to pass in our lives. That's why it's always best to do our best to make sure these plans are aligned with God's heart in the very beginning so we can avoid potential disappointments in the future. I believe that if we all did a better job at this then there would be less cases of depression and fewer frustrated people in the world. Removing un-submitted expectations that fall outside of the scope of God's will for our lives would ultimately help us avoid falling into these pitfalls of wounded emotions.

The next mistake I made was not trusting my own instincts or rather the signs that God would often times send. Know that no matter situation you are facing, God is never silent towards it. At times, He will use that small inner voice within you, which I believe everyone has but for believers, it is known to be the inner workings of the Holy Spirit. 1 Corinthians 2:9-10 says "...As it is written: "No eye has seen, no ear has heard, no mind has conceived what God has prepared for those who love him-- but God has revealed it to us by his Spirit." As stated in previous chapters, God wants you to know His will concerning your situation, and will many times go through great lengths to try and reveal it to you. However, walking in deception will cause you to miss out on it. I can still recall the numerous signs telling me that the man I believed to be my husband really in fact wasn't but was only meant to be a friend. Things would happen in our relationship that would make me feel uneasy but I would just convince myself that these things would change. Yet, another mistake one can experience in the midst of deception—choosing to avoid/neglect the obvious red flags.

Famous poet/author Maya Angelou has often said "The first time someone shows you who they are, believe them." Time and time again it was shown that we weren't exactly the best fit for one another. And what did I do? Totally, neglected it and in some cases, even justified it but again this is what deception does. It got to the point where I convinced myself that my inclination to marry this man was derived from God and as such nothing else mattered. Now I feel the need to point out here that it wasn't that I was dealing with a bad person. In fact, he was absolutely great! However, he wasn't the one God designed specifically for me. Likewise, you may find yourself in a similar situation today. Perhaps, it may not be a relationship per say. Maybe it's a job, maybe it's a decision, or maybe it's a ministry and God is saying yeah that's good but that's not exactly what I have in mind for you. Do not allow the deception to get you outside of the will of God. Believe me, this is a very dangerous place to be. Not only can you delay or potentially totally miss out on God's best for you, but you also run the risk of losing valuable time in the process. Indeed, I cannot stress enough how dangerous deception can be in hindering purpose and destiny.

### Reflection Point

Make the decision today to not believe the lies you are told—-whether as a child or now as an adult. The fact is that there are going to be countless lies told to you, but you will never know that they are lies unless you first know what the truth is. John 8:32 says that "you will know the truth, and the truth will set you free." According to John 14:6, Jesus is the way, the truth, and the life and no one can come to the Father except through him. If you don't know him, I will encourage you to get to know him. If you do know him, I encourage you to get to know him more for the more you know him the more you'll experience freedom through Him.

## Roadblock II: Excuses

"Excuses are a crutch for the uncommitted"
- Pastor Isha Edmondson

The next common roadblock has to do with one I've grown all too familiar with—Excuse making. In the Webster's dictionary one of the definitions given for excuse is "something offered as justification or as grounds for being excused." In other words, making excuses can easily be a way to explain away or find reason why it's okay to not follow through with a given action. It somehow makes it acceptable (or at least in our own eyes) to not be proactive, and in the process produces a lazy mentality that limits us more than it supposedly liberates us. I can recall a point in time when I could have had a master's degree in excuse making because that is how often I used them. Then my Pastor preached a mini-series on excuse making and it changed my life forever. Though I won't go so far as to say it happened over night, the revelation that came forth through that teaching stuck with me and has progressively changed the way I see excuse making over time.

# The Victim's Mentality

I think many of us have become great at playing the blame game including myself. Somehow it seems easier to pass the buck than to take responsibility for one's own actions. Have you ever met someone who specializes in being the victim? Unfortunately, I've had the opportunity of crossing paths with many who fall in this category and it can be quite frustrating trying to walk them to victory when all they can see in their mind is VICTIM. I guess perhaps the saddest part about it is, many times, the person doesn't even realize it even when they are in it knee deep. In fact, typically they're completely oblivious to it and will probably give you the ole deer in the headlights look if you even suggest it to them as a possibility. Still, in order to move on freely into one's destiny it must be dealt with or else it would only hinder and avert progress.

I recall not too long ago having a conversation with my half-brother whom I share the same dad with. He was sharing with me how he felt that life had dealt him a terrible hand and that was the reason why he was unable to get a break in life. He proceeded to talk about how our father was never there for any of us, which was true and how he never modeled a good picture of fatherhood, which was true as well. However, I also pointed out to him that this didn't have to stop him from being there for his own young children and doing for them what was never done for us. Additionally, I shared with him how much of life is what you make it and the beauty of it is that no matter how far you may go down, getting up is always an option. Still, he continued on about how things were over for him because of his prison record and that no job would ever want him. In response to that I told him that we all make mistakes but we don't have to allow those mistakes to define us nor limit us. That ultimately, where there is a will, there is always a way and the possibility of starting afresh and anew.

## Reflection Point

So often the victim's mentality has us focus on all that we don't have instead of the possibilities of what we can have. I encourage you today to make it a point to stop telling God how big your challenges are and tell your challenges how big your God is!

### Roadblock III: Pride

*"Pride goes before destruction, a haughty spirit before a fall."—Proverbs 16:18*

The third roadblock to destiny we'll discuss is the one which often hides and that is...Pride. Pride is the opposite of humility and thus often causes one to be puffed up and haughty. It involves an unwillingness to submit to God and a belief that one knows better than He does. I would venture to say that it's something that we all struggle with, and perhaps, one of the best ways to overcome it is through the realization of how frail we are in comparison to the Almighty God.

*"For he knows how weak we are; he remembers we are only dust." –Psalm 103:14 (NLT)*

One of the most liberating places to be in life is knowing you don't need to have all of the answers. In essence, it takes the pressure off of you and places it where it belongs—on God. Who better to have to handle it then someone who is more than equipped? Whenever, I'm battling with the desire to take things into my own hands, I like to refer to one of my favorite chapters found in Psalm 131 (NIV). It goes like this:

*"My heart is not proud, Lord,*
*my eyes are not haughty;*
*I do not concern myself with great matters*
*or things too wonderful for me.*
*But I have calmed and quieted myself,*
*I am like a weaned child with its mother;*
*like a weaned child I am content.*
*(Insert Your Name Here), put your hope in the Lord*
*Both now and forevermore."*

This is how God wants us to approach life and the challenges it brings. While it's easy to depend on our own skills, knowledge, and abilities, God wants us to lean on Him instead. This is why Proverbs 3:5-6 gives instruction to "Trust in the LORD with all your heart and lean not on your own understanding; in all your ways submit to him, and he will make your paths straight." I am convinced that many of the problems we face in life often come from our unwillingness to do exactly this--trust and submit.

Recently, I was reading a TGIF devotional by Author Os Hillman, and in this devotional he made reference to the story of Moses as he led the children of Israel to the Promise Land. (Please see excerpt below):

"The people of Israel were complaining that they did not have water to drink. It was another of many tests for Israel. Moses inquired of God and God said, "...Speak to that rock before their eyes and it will pour out its water" (Num. 20:8a). Moses, in his frustration and anger with the people, began to act on his own and made a strategic mistake. Instead of speaking to the rock, he struck the rock twice with his staff...He used his staff, the symbol of his work life as a shepherd, to force the provision."

Despite Moses clear disobedience God still allowed the water to flow out. However, Moses forfeited his opportunity to enter into the Promised Land with the rest of the camp. While he came close to experiencing the full manifestation of God's promises, he fell short of it simply due to his own self will. Wouldn't it hurt knowing you've done all of these wonderful things in life, or specifically for the kingdom of God to only fall short of accomplishing your true purpose? The truth is that it happens to many people all of the time. They go throughout their lives doing all of these GOOD things, but because it's not GOD-ordained things, they miss out on true fulfillment and satisfaction in life. They become busy with just doing instead of being the person God has called them to be in life. Let me ask you…is this the kind of life you would imagine yourself living? If the answer to this question is no, then I encourage you today to make the choice to trust and submit.

Do not become like Saul before he became known as Paul. Up until his conversion he fought against the very One who could truly help him. This is why in Acts 26:14, we hear God say to him: "Saul, Saul, why are you persecuting me? It is useless for you to fight against my will (NLT)." I've said it before and I will say it again, IT IS ABSOLUTELY POINTLESS TO BUCK UP AGAINST GOD'S WILL. Regardless, of what we do or don't do—God's will is going to happen by choice or by force so why not make a decision to flow with it and bypass the consequences associated with rebelling.

Easier said than done right? I must admit, I've had numerous occasions to learn this the hard way. Just recently, I found myself fighting against God's will in the area of finances and employment. After being laid off of work, I turned to

44

unemployment to help pay my bills while I went back to school. Once unemployment was abruptly cut off, I was in a place where I had to either get a job or struggle. Of course, like anyone else, I decided that getting a job would be the most ideal because, let's face it, there's nothing appealing about struggle—at least not to me. When it comes to God; however, there seems to be another story. While God does not intend for his children to struggle, He, more than anyone, understands and places great value on the good that comes out of it.

## Learning Sufficiency in God

*"The more you lose yourself in something bigger than yourself, the more energy you will have."*

-Norman Vincent Peale

Ultimately, I believe God had to take me through this season to teach me a very valuable lesson in humility. For so many years I had learned to rely on myself to get things and make things happen. Since the age of 16, I was relatively on my own so being able to work and provide for myself had become a common thing for me. I had grown quite accustomed to it. Even transitioning to unemployment itself was challenging yet bearable because I knew I had paid taxes into this fund for many years, so in a way I had worked for it. Then, when this source was completely cut off I had to rely on nothing but God. I felt like someone had snatched away my most beloved childhood stuffed animal. You know the one that becomes a security blanket sometimes even up to adolescent years. It was totally different for me and extremely uncomfortable. I had to quickly realize that God was my source and that unemployment was merely a resource.

45

For a while, I fought it and went out job hunting anyway. Still, it was to no avail. Although organizations were interested in me and I had several interviews, the situation never turned out to be what I thought it was and I ended up having to walk away. In addition to this, I always felt that uneasiness that I was stepping outside of the confines of God's will for my life for that particular season. Truth be told, I was because God had made it clear to me that He did not want me to work right away but that my focus had to be on finishing this book. So, I relented. I stopped the job search and turned my attentions to the book and to the plethora of other things I already had on my plate. Not only did I find this process to be extremely humbling but somehow it had also succeeded in increasing my faith walk in ways like I had never experienced before. For over two months I went without any income at all. There was no savings to fall back on and no revenue from my business. It was only the grace of God that enabled me to keep every bill paid and not miss a meal in the process. I can remember times when I received unexpected checks or money, or the time when my friend and I were sitting at a restaurant and the manager came over to us and handed us each a free tray of their famous nuggets—not just any tray but a catering tray which fed fifteen or more people—the sauce was included and it was absolutely FREE! The way God showed out and still continues to show out is absolutely extraordinary. In many ways, it reminds me of the account in the Bible where Abraham thought he had to sacrifice his only begotten son Isaac, only to see that God was just trying to position him to experience his divine provision.

Genesis 22:9-14

*9 When they reached the place God had told him about, Abraham built an altar there and arranged the wood on it. He bound his son Isaac and laid him on the altar, on top of the wood. 10 Then he reached out his hand and took the knife to slay his son. 11 But the angel of the Lord called out to him from heaven, "Abraham! Abraham!" "Here I am," he replied.*

*12 "Do not lay a hand on the boy," he said. "Do not do anything to him. Now I know that you fear God, because you have not withheld from me your son, your only son."*

*13 Abraham looked up and there in a thicket he saw a ram[a] caught by its horns. He went over and took the ram and sacrificed it as a burnt offering instead of his son. 14 So Abraham called that place The Lord Will Provide. And to this day it is said, "On the mountain of the Lord it will be provided."*

I would venture to say that if Abraham had never gone through this experience, he may never have been able to experience God as Jehovah Jireh—a God who provides. Likewise, it was through my recent financial setback, along with other challenging circumstances that I, too, have come to experience God as a God who provides. As such, it has enabled me to place more dependency on Him and less dependency on myself.

Recently, during a conversation with my good friend, Timothy, we spoke about the challenges that can often be associated with this trying yet necessary process. He was learning how to trust God more concerning his ambitions, drive, and success; whereas, I was discovering how to trust God for my basic necessities. Being very driven and self-motivated doers we both found the overall process to be quite humbling. For him, the struggle was being able to center his desires and drive in God. Lately, he found himself struggling with the motivation to carry out certain tasks. No matter how much he tried to push through, feelings of defeat and apathy seemed to always creep in. As one who has always been a go getter in life, this was very upsetting

47

and unsettling for him. Finally, together we were able to draw the conclusion that God was allowing him to go through this process so that he could reposition his confidence and motivation in Him. In other words, God was teaching him how to go from being self-sufficient to being God sufficient. While Timothy could normally breeze through life using his own abilities and personal drive to achieve success, he was now being challenged to depend on God to accomplish the same. Talk about being humbled!

The greatest part about it all is that God will do much more and accomplish much greater than we ever could operating out of our own strength! God was only trying to position Timothy to receive a greater level of grace and provision for his life. In the same way, God has been positioning me to receive a greater level of grace and provision in the area of finances. Although I have always recognized God as my true source, it wasn't until I had to walk through this process that the true revelation of it really resonated within me. That being said, I can now more honestly say that He has brought me to a place of God-sufficiency.

II Corinthians 12:7-10 (NLV)

*"...Even though I have received such wonderful revelations from God. So to keep me from becoming proud, I was given a thorn in my flesh, a messenger from Satan to torment me and keep me from becoming proud. Three different times I begged the Lord to take it away. Each time he said, "My grace is all you need. My power works best in weakness." So now I am glad to boast about my weaknesses, so that the power of Christ can work through me. That's why I take pleasure in my weaknesses and in the insults, hardships, persecutions, and troubles that I suffer for Christ. For when I am weak, then I AM STRONG."*

## Reflection Point

Take a few minutes to reflect and consider whether there are any areas of your life that are currently un-submitted or un-surrendered to God. If so, take the next few minutes to repent and place them before God. Then meditate on the following scripture:

1 Peter 5-7

*...All of you, clothe yourselves with humility toward one another, because, "God opposes the proud but shows favor to the humble." Humble yourselves, therefore, under God's mighty hand, that he may lift you up in due time. Cast all your anxiety on him because he cares for you.*

# The Great Fall

*"Do you wish to rise? Begin by descending. You plan a tower that will pierce the clouds? Lay first the foundation of humility."*
--Saint Augustine

Often, another useful tool to bring us from pride to humility is falling flat on our face, or in other words, coming to the end of yourself. I believe that just about everyone gets to a point in life where they feel as if they hit rock bottom. For me, this point has come and gone several times but more recently it seems to have come and literally pitched a tent. It all started about a year and a half ago when I received my first ever (and hopefully last) pink slip from my employer. Interestingly enough I was somewhat prepared for it and even had peace about it before it happened, so much so, I was able to rejoice in the situation despite knowing I was about to lose my job. Nonetheless, this could never have prepared me for the road that lied ahead. In the next year and a half I would soon find myself hit with many ups and downs, highs and lows, tough decision making, and dare I say the word—Detours.

Like many of us in life, I was fooled into believing that if I just did really well in school and worked hard in life I would be bound for success. This faulty belief came crashing down on me when the rug was pulled out from under me and I suddenly found myself going from making over $50k a year to about half of that, to finally having no income at all. The most challenging part was that I still had a home, a car, and all the bills that came along with it. So what was I to do? Well, the only response I could have was to trust in God and sometimes this is easier said than done. I remember the day when I found out that they were abruptly cutting funds for unemployment, and with very short notice, my checks would stop. I recall feeling helpless, caught off guard, and hoodwinked all at once.

You see, I was led to believe that as long as I remained in school I would be covered until my program ended. Since I'm always about furthering my education; I took advantage of this opportunity by making the decision to pursue my doctorate along with a couple of other related certificate programs. Little did I know that the regulation would change in a blink of an eye, but I guess such is life, right? So, all in one shot, I was informed that my only income would be cut off, I would be forced to apply for public assistance, and in order to be eligible I needed to pull out of my doctoral program.

Heartbreaking… could not begin to describe the feelings that I felt at this time. I can remember sitting in my car after it was all said and done and just looking out the window with the blankest of stares. You know the one where you've officially timed out and you feel like you're kind of having an outer body experience—as if your mind has somehow drifted off into space and you now find yourself struggling to grasp it back. Well, that's pretty much where I was, but thanks to God I didn't stay there. A few short minutes later, the Lord began to minister reassurance to me that He was with me through this process and that there was purpose in what I was going through. He told me that there were also many others going through the very same or similar situation and that the difference for me was that at the end of the day at least I had HOPE. Even though I needed to be reminded of this now and then, the fact is that I knew that ultimately God was in control. And although at times, it hurt really bad and I emphasize really bad, deep down I knew it was for a greater good. Well, at least, this is what God revealed to me.

Then as if on key, shortly after getting this revelation, I was prompted to check my voicemail. To my surprise I discovered a message from a lady who I hadn't spoken with in over a year. Initially, she had reached out to me after reading an article describing a job support network I was working on establishing for the unemployed and underemployed. This particular day she was calling to ask for my help in getting some resources to a group of police officers who were about to experience a similar lay off situation. Instantly, I knew that God was confirming the word He had just given to me. I realized at that moment, the situation I was going through had little to do with me and much more to do with the people who needed to hear my story and also experience the compassion that I could give only after having gone through such a great loss myself. Ironically enough, the lady I spoke with that day, although not even knowing me on a personal level, felt exactly the same way.

So why am I sharing all of this you may ask? Well, I believe that are several points illustrated in this story. The first point is nothing in life is ever guaranteed except for salvation. Indeed, everything else can be subject to change, whether it is job status, relationship status, economic status…and the list could go on and on. While I would have liked to have believed that success was a formula easily obtained by following a couple of tested and proven steps, the reality is that true success really has nothing to do with a checklist at all. In fact, true success, at least for me, couldn't even be achieved until the task list was gone. For it was in its absence that I began to see what really mattered in life—not the fancy jobs, big homes and nice cars but it is the ability to impact someone's life for the better. That, to me is true success. To be able to live life fulfilled knowing that someone's life, situation, or predicament is better because of you and your mere existence. I believe no amount of money or health benefit package could ever compare to that. Think about it…you never hear about those things being read during a eulogy, but what you do hear about is all the lives the person has impacted and all the deeds they've done that have gone a long way. This is lasting and eternal, while all of the other stuff is simply temporal and can easily fade away much like a trend that has outstayed its welcome.

## Still Falling

It is believed that one of the darkest moments of the day is right before dawn. Some may look at seasons like this and think that they have fallen from grace but just the opposite is happening. You're actually falling into grace for it's in such times as these which develop true dependence on the Father. Often it takes trials and set-backs in life to bring you to a place of humility and reliance on God. In other words, you have to come to the end of your rope before you can truly cling onto that which provides true support and stability—God.

Recently, a good friend of mine shared with me his experience with one of the greatest falls of his life but perhaps not the type you would imagine—sky diving. Could you envision jumping out of a plane two miles in the air and being suspended into a free fall drop of 120 miles an hour? Nope, neither can I but that is exactly what he did, and he did it willingly! What would make someone take such a risky and somewhat scary jump out of an airplane you may wonder? Well, I would suppose the same thing that would propel one forth into their destiny— courage and faith. When you truly consider it, launching out knee deep into your destiny can almost be just as nerve racking as looking out of the airplane 10,000 feet below you and choosing to take that jump even when you can't see from afar exactly what you're jumping into. In both cases, it can be pretty much a blur. Nonetheless, he had the courage and faith to take that bold step (or should I say leap) that day. Interestingly enough, what I found to be even more surprising about it all is just how liberating it turned out to be for him. Who would have thought falling from the sky faster than a speeding train would be liberating but amazingly it is. I think, in part, it has to do with the ability to fully let go and surrender all control because let's face it, aside from pulling the string to the parachute, there's not much you can do while falling 8,000 feet in the sky.

Life can seem very much like this once you've made the decision to go full speed ahead in your passion and purpose. There are times when the fear of the unknown will try to grip you and hinder you from taking that anticipated leap but it is important to remember at these times that this leap is never the end but rather the beginning. Although you may not always know exactly what you're getting into, you can jump confidently in knowing that no matter how distant or far off your destination may appear, you are still guaranteed to reach land at some point and with the right faith and positioning you may find yourself landing square on your feet.

The key is to not give up...no matter how tough and uncertain things may appear you have to remember that things will get better. Just as what goes up must come down; the same can be said of the very low points we experience. Many times, you will only go up from there. As I write this I am reminded of a recent blog written by my good friend Tene' Aiken. As an aspiring artist and entrepreneur Tene' has experienced more than her share of ups and downs in the pursuit of her destiny, and I believe that the following excerpt from her blog gives a little insight to this experience:

"I have learned that on this journey to leaving this awesome legacy that lies within me, there are plenty of unexpected turns. I could either end the journey short of making it to the finish line in order to avoid those unexpected turns or I could navigate my way through the unexpected turns with tenacity. I choose the later of the two. There may be struggles, success may look different than I thought, and things may not always go according to scheduled plans, but at least I am fervently going after what I know I was placed here on this Earth to do!"

Wow...what a powerful statement! It makes me reminiscent of the famous quote by Henry David Thoreau which says "Go confidently in the direction of your dreams. Live the life you have imagined." In order to live the life you always imagined, there will many times be risks to take but if you stay your course you will see that it's more than worth it! Remember low risk, low reward....high risk, high reward. Follow your dreams!

### From the Pit to the Palace

One of my favorite stories in the Bible is the story of Joseph. Not only was Joseph an avid dreamer, but like many other dreamers, he experienced the topsy turvy process often associated with accepting the call of his dream. For starters, upon sharing the dream with his brothers and father, he received instant ridicule and rebuke (Genesis 37:5-10). Verses 8 and 10 tell us that his brothers hated him because of his dream and his father questioned the soundness of it. The reality is that not everyone is going to be happy about the great and wondrous things that God intends to do through your life, especially if they have yet to see great things manifest in their own lives. Much like what Joseph experienced, some people may ridicule you; talk behind your back, or just straight out try to convince you that it's not worth all the trouble of you pursuing the dream at all. In such cases, you must make up in your mind in advance to silence out the naysayers and keep it moving. In other cases, it may be wise to be selective in whom you share your dreams with in the first place, recognizing that not everyone will be able to handle it.

Such was the case with Joseph's brothers. Hearing his dream ate away at them so much so that they conspired to kill him— their very own flesh and blood. However, thank God, they did not follow through with their plan and instead opted to throw him into a pit and sell him into slavery.

Genesis 37: 23-24

*"So when Joseph came to his brothers, they stripped him of his robe, the robe of many colors that he wore. And they took him and threw him into a pit. The pit was empty; there was no water in it."(ESV)*

I would imagine that EMPTY all but described what Joseph had to be feeling during this time in his life. Here he had just received these visions of the promises God had for him and instead of things seeming to move forward; it appeared that they were now taking a nose dive down ward. His life had literally turned upside down and it happened overnight.

Perhaps, in some ways you can relate to this place in Joseph's life. I know that I certainly can. Sometimes, it can seem as if just when things are turning in your favor, all hell breaks out but really that's just a clear indication that you are on the right track. This is exactly what happened to me when I decided to write this book. Although I was already unemployed at the start, I had learned to live within my means and was at a place of financial comfort when all of a sudden a week after this new journey began I received the letter in the mail informing me that my entire financial situation was about to change and change for the worse. This could have been a prime opportunity for me to say, you know maybe I had it all wrong, perhaps this book project isn't a good idea after all. Maybe that dream I had was just something I ate the night before and perhaps I should just give up on the whole idea and find a full time job. But that's not what God told me to do, so I had to ride it out. The same can go with you. No matter how frustrating things may appear, remember that there is always a greater glory to be revealed.

Romans 8:18

*I consider that our present sufferings are not worth comparing with the glory that will be revealed in us.*

Think about what would have happened if Joseph simply threw in the towel right then and there. What if he said to himself, "well, I guess the pit was really what God may have had in mind so I mine as well get comfortable here and just accept that this is where I am." What if he decided to have a big "woe is me" party and put the rest of his life on cruise control, no longer choosing to take an active role in his life but instead moping around in defeat? Well, I will tell you what could have happened. For starters, he probably wouldn't have experienced as much success and favor having that kind of attitude. Genesis 39:4 says, "Joseph found favor in his eyes and became his attendant. Potiphar put him in charge of his household, and he entrusted to his care everything he owned." An unmotivated person who has given up on themselves and the call of God on their life will more than likely not gain the attention nor experience the kind of success that Joseph did to put him in this position. Nor would have they probably have handled themselves the way Joseph did when he was falsely accused and placed in prison (or shall we just call it the pit).

For some people, this would have been the last straw. While they may have been able to handle one setback, not being fully persuaded and rooted in their purpose may have caused them to give up after the next one. I bet even Joseph may have felt the pressure at some point and perhaps even thought something like, wow, God it's one thing after another...can I catch a break? Nonetheless, Joseph never allowed these setbacks to bring him down and just as he prospered in Potiphar's house so he prospered in prison.

Genesis 39:22-23

*So the warden put Joseph in charge of all those held in the prison, and he was made responsible for all that was done there. The warden paid no attention to anything under Joseph's care, because the Lord was with Joseph and gave him success in whatever he did.*

You see, Joseph showed that he understood the important lesson of learning how to be content in his situation. In other words, he did not allow the change in his circumstances to change his attitude towards things. Just as he acted within Potiphar's house, so he did in the prison. He put into practice the message Paul preached in Philippians 4:12 when he said: "I know what it is to be in need, and I know what it is to have plenty. I have learned the secret of being content in any and every situation, whether well fed or hungry, whether living in plenty or in want." Joseph remained consistent; consistency is key when you're going after your purpose and destiny.

I recall having a recent conversation with a very good friend of mine. I was sharing with him my struggles in being able to write this book and how challenging it was to reveal some of the things I was currently experiencing, particularly the financial woes. In response to this he said to me, "Keanna, I think you may be struggling with this because you're focusing too much on where you are now. You see yourself in the pit and yes that may be where God has you at the moment, but that's not where you are going to stay. You have to believe and focus on the fact that God is preparing you for and propelling you towards the palace. So, although you are in the pit right now, you need to write as if you were in the palace." These words helped changed my entire outlook on things and freed me up to flow in more transparency while understanding that my past or present don't define who I am but simply refine who I become. Shortly after this, I listened to my pastor preach two sermons almost back to back and refer to something very similar. He made reference to the fact that sometimes in life you will find yourself in the pit, but nonetheless, praise like you are in the palace. Talk about confirmation!

Moreover, this is a message I believe we all must cling to no matter what life may bring you or where it may take you. You must believe in the dream that God has placed within you and believe in your ability to accomplish it. No matter how tough things got for Joseph, still he never stopped dreaming and perhaps what is even more awesome is that in the process of waiting for God to reveal and manifest his dream, he helped reveal and provide solutions to other people's dreams.

Genesis 41:25-40

*25 Then Joseph said to Pharaoh, "The dreams of Pharaoh are one and the same. God has revealed to Pharaoh what he is about to do. 26 The seven good cows are seven years, and the seven good heads of grain are seven years; it is one and the same dream. 27 The seven lean, ugly cows that came up afterward are seven years, and so are the seven worthless heads of grain scorched by the east wind: They are seven years of famine.*

*28 "It is just as I said to Pharaoh: God has shown Pharaoh what he is about to do. 29 Seven years of great abundance are coming throughout the land of Egypt, 30 but seven years of famine will follow them. Then all the abundance in Egypt will be forgotten, and the famine will ravage the land. 31 The abundance in the land will not be remembered, because the famine that follows it will be so severe. 32 The reason the dream was given to Pharaoh in two forms is that the matter has been firmly decided by God, and God will do it soon.*

*33 "And now let Pharaoh look for a discerning and wise man and put him in charge of the land of Egypt. 34 Let Pharaoh appoint commissioners over the land to take a fifth of the harvest of Egypt during the seven years of abundance. 35 They should collect all the food of these good years that are coming and store up the grain under the authority of Pharaoh, to be kept in the cities for food. 36 This food should be held in reserve for the country, to be used during the seven years of famine that will come upon Egypt, so that the country may not be ruined by the famine."*

*37 The plan seemed good to Pharaoh and to all his officials. 38 So Pharaoh asked them, "Can we find anyone like this man, one in whom is the spirit of God?"*

*39 Then Pharaoh said to Joseph, "Since God has made all this known to you, there is no one so discerning and wise as you. 40 You shall be in charge of my palace, and all my people are to submit to your orders. Only with respect to the throne will I be greater than you."*


Joseph's ability to remain consistent and never give up, allowed him to become a solution for someone else which then set him up to his rightful position as second in command to Pharaoh. He had indeed finally made it to the palace, but he did it not moaning and groaning but instead believing and sowing. Psalm 126:5-6 says that "those who sow with tears will reap with songs of joy. Those who go out weeping, carrying seed to sow,

61

will return with songs of joy, carrying sheaves with them." One of the greatest lessons I have learned in my own pit experience is that ..."It is not about me" but it's about God's glory being revealed. Ironically, even during my most difficult financial woes, I still found myself sowing more than I have during more prosperous seasons. I discovered that it wasn't the quantity that mattered as much as the quality. In other words, the fact that I didn't have a whole lot to sow didn't outweigh my willingness to sow liberally out of the little that I did have.

This principle turned out to be valuable for several reasons:

1. It allowed me to focus less on my own circumstances as I stepped out of my current situation and placed my focus on doing something good for someone else.

2. It created even more dependence on God because as I gave out of the little that I did have, I had to trust that God was going to restore it, so that I would never run out myself. Thus, it increased my level of faith in God's ability to supply. It's the open hand concept that the more my hand is open to give, it's also open to receive.

3. I was able to tap into the law of reciprocity. This ties into my previous point that the more you give the more you receive and that's exactly what happened. I was able to see God provide in so many awesome ways because I tapped into a law. This does not always have to relate over to money but it can involve any form of sacrifice being made for someone else. I have often heard my pastor say that when we are willing to be provision for someone else's vision, then God will send someone to provision for ours.

4. It allowed me to display obedience and reap the rewards that come along with it. Isaiah 1:19 tells us that "If you are willing and obedient, you will eat the best from the land." Many times, God will require certain things from us during our pit experiences that will not only test our willingness to trust Him but also show whether or not we are willing to still do what we need to do even when the odds are stacked up against and we do not necessarily feel like it. Ultimately, it leads to the fifth and final point.

5. Character—usually going through these situations allows us to build character. There is a saying that skills and abilities can get you certain places in life, but it will be your integrity that keeps you there. I believe that part of the reason it took Joseph around thirteen years to see his dream manifested is due to God's desire to make sure he was adequately prepared for it. Ultimately, it came down to his character. Unfortunately, character is not something you can learn in a classroom or through reading the hottest and latest inspirational books but it is something that is learned in the battlefields of life. It's the decisions we choose to make even when no one else seems to be looking at us—it's the stuff that true champions are made of.

Moreover, I'm convinced that the development of character is one of the main reasons why we often experience so many detours and challenges in life. You see, while we are often more interested in getting to the destination, God is more concerned with what we learn during the process. There is an interesting quote by a man named Ursula K. Le Guin that says, "It is good to have an end to journey towards; but it is the journey that matters in the end". God had to ensure that once he brought

Joseph to the ultimate place he had for Him that He wouldn't get puffed up and forget who had positioned him there in the first place. Even more, it was important that once Joseph got to that place that he still did the things that God would require of him, which specifically included taking care of his family—including the very brothers who first betrayed him.

Genesis 50:19-21

*But Joseph said to them, "Don't be afraid. Am I in the place of God? You intended to harm me, but God intended it for good to accomplish what is now being done, the saving of many lives. So then, don't be afraid. I will provide for you and your children." And he reassured them and spoke kindly to them.*

The many detours Joseph experienced ultimately brought him to a place of humility and compassion which allowed him to see the manifestation of his dreams for what it really was—an opportunity to do good and bring glory to God's kingdom. Who knows if the conviction to do this would have been so great if he only had to skip down easy street to get there?

### Reflection Point

Are you currently experiencing setbacks and challenges that appear to be out of your control? I know that the natural tendency during this is to question God and sometimes even mope and complain. However, I encourage you to begin looking at the situation differently form here out and instead of asking God: Why, Lord, why am I going through this? Begin to ask him: What is it Lord that you are trying to show me, teach me, or cultivate through me during this process.

Remember the longer it takes to get this, the longer you may find yourself in that detour, so don't delay.

# Strategic Positioning

*"You will not have to fight this battle. Take up your positions; stand firm and see the deliverance the Lord will give you..."*

-2 Chronicles 20:17

Once you are able to get to the point of true submission before God and get aligned with His will, then God can really begin to work out things on your behalf. All too often, we make the mistake of trying to force our way through doors when God is saying to just stay in His will and He will strategically position you right where you need to be. It reminds me of the story of how God elevated David. Some may think that I'm referring to His victory over Goliath but actually it came even prior to this.

1 Samuel 16:13-19 (NIV)

"So Samuel took the horn of oil and anointed him in the presence of his brothers, and from that day on the Spirit of the LORD came upon David in power. Samuel then went to Ramah. Now the Spirit of the LORD had departed from Saul, and an evil spirit from the LORD tormented him. Saul's attendants said to him, 'See, an evil spirit from God is tormenting you. Let our lord command his servants here to search for someone who can play the harp. He will play when the evil spirit from God comes upon you, and you will feel better.' So Saul said to his attendants, 'Find someone who plays well and bring him to me.' One of the servants answered, 'I have seen a son of Jesse of Bethlehem who knows how to play the harp. He is a brave man and a warrior. He speaks well and is a fine-looking man. And the LORD is with him.' Then Saul sent messengers to Jesse and said, 'Send me your son David, who is with the sheep.'

First, we see that in verse 13 God sent Samuel to anoint David. Another word that can be used in place of the word anoint is blessed, so in other words David received God's blessing to accomplish His will. One of the key indications that God has blessed you to do a specific work is His empowering presence on your life to accomplish it. As discussed earlier in the book, you may not even be walking in the actual calling/purpose yet but the signs that it exists should still be evident in your life. For instance, if you believe that God has called you to be a counselor but you can't stand people and have a very short tolerance level, then nine times out of ten you may have misheard him on that one. Likewise, if you feel strongly that you're supposed to be a singer/songstress but whenever you break out in a melody people go running and screaming in the opposite direction, then perhaps you should consider a re-evaluation of that as well.

Shortly after David is anointed we see a strange string of events occur. First, Samuel leaves him. I could only imagine what could have been going through David's mind at the time. (Wait a minute you just did this grandiose thing in my life and now you're leaving!) In fact, I believe that is how we feel sometimes in our relationship with God. One moment we feel like we are on cloud nine with Him gaining all of this new found revelation and hearing from Him at greater levels then before and then the next minute there's complete silence. Soon we begin to wonder if He's even there at all. The truth remains that He is indeed there. He said that He would never leave us nor forsake us (Hebrews 13:5). However, this doesn't negate the fact that there will be times where we won't always feel His presence; for it's in times like these that we have to respond off of what we know and not what we feel. To put it simply, God has to remove the security blanket or whatever crutch that exists in our lives so that what we really believe can come to the surface. For often, it's not on the mountaintop but in the valley that we discover where our faith truly lies.

After Samuel departs, the scene switches to Saul, who is the present King over Israel. In the next following verses we find out that Saul is being tormented by an evil Spirit sent from the Lord. You may be wondering why God would even allow an evil spirit to torment the same man He once anointed as king. Well, it's quite simple. Saul, once the rightful ruler of Israel abused his authority when he stepped outside the confines of God's command. From that day forward he then continued to lead as king but with a pink slip because in God's eyes He was fired and David was now the designated one to take the throne . Thus, when God sent the evil spirit to Saul, He did it knowing that David would be the one they would call on to be a solution to Saul's dilemma. You see sometimes God will create a challenge in someone's life just so He can raise up someone like you to be the answer. Proverbs 18:16 tells us that "A man's gift makes room for him, and brings him before great men." God knew that this would be an opportunity for David to gain favor with King Saul and eventually gain access to him as if he were one of his sons. You see if David had tried to force his way into the king's chamber, it wouldn't have worked but since God orchestrated everything, it set him up right where he needed to be.

For many years I saw God do this for me in the area of employment. As much as I would try to make things happen, it would never seem to pan out but when I placed it in God's hands it always resulted in a positive outcome. I witnessed one of the first occurrences when I began researching for a graduate internship. The non-profit organization that I had hoped to get into was no longer accepting new interns, so I found myself only weeks out from my final semester with not one prospect for an internship. Stressed was perhaps an understatement for how I felt especially since completing an internship was critical to me graduating that upcoming Spring. Somehow, the director at my work study program found out about my dilemma and immediately went to work on my behalf. The next thing I knew I had two internship opportunities lined up. Talk about having God shut one door only to open up two better ones. Ultimately, I had to choose from interning with a state senator or with the Chief Operating Officer for the City of Camden. I ended up choosing the latter and it definitely paid off. Not only did I gain great experience but I was also able to establish great connections that remain even to this day.

Amazingly, things didn't stop there. Once I finished out my last semester of graduate school, God told me that I didn't need to stress and worry about landing a job because He was going to bring the job to me. Still fired up from seeing how He worked out the last situation I got really excited about seeing what God was going to do next. I may have applied to a job here and there but ultimately I trusted that God was going to take care of it. But then the strangest thing happened—nothing. That's right, nothing seemed to come through and at this point weeks had passed and finally months. It was now seven months since I had graduated and six months since God had given me that revelation but there still were no prospects in sight, so I did what any other casual Christian would do—I panicked. I began to apply to as many jobs as I could and attended job fair after job fair. Finally, I had found a job that seemed to be just right for me. It was a Human Resources position for the federal government's office of personnel. After reading the description for the job, I just knew that God had tailor made this job just for me. So, I tweaked my resume, developed a cover letter and got my application in before the prescribed deadline in January. Then, I put my faith out there and waited but again nothing happened. Finally, about a month later I called to check on the status of my application and was informed that I didn't make the cut. In my mind all I could hear was the final door closing in my face...boom!

A few days later out of nowhere I received a call from a company in which I had interviewed with about seven months ago. To give a good backdrop I have to rewind back to that past June when God spoke to me about the job situation. At the time I was still working as a graduate intern for a research institute. It just so happened that that following month they were tasked with implementing a three-day seminar for the Executive Board of Camden. In addition to utilizing the consultants from the organization, the project also utilized one of my previous professors from the Public Policy department. I was then asked to come alongside him to assist with carrying out his research but to my surprise he thought enough of my ability that he asked me to not only conduct research for it, but to also present a portion of it as well. I knew right away how much of a grand opportunity this was from me.

To my excitement the presentation was a great success! Many of the directors commented on how well they felt I had done and how much they had enjoyed the presentation, but that wasn't even the best part by far. The part I've been working my way up to is that shortly thereafter one of the directors approached me directly, shared with me how impressed he was with my abilities and told me that I was just the type of person they needed for their organization. The next day I was called in for my first interview. There it was reinforced that I was the one for the job but there was one problem...the funding for the position hadn't come through yet and even more, they had no idea of when it would. Eventually, a month had passed then two and I had begun to convince myself that although I initially thought that this was God's promise coming to pass, I then began to question if I had heard it correctly in the first place. It finally took between six to seven months for me to see that it really was what God had said all along, for I got the job and it was done without having to go through the normal process of finding one. Just like He said, it had come to me and it had come right in the nick of time just as the last door was being shut in my face!

Ultimately, this taught me a valuable lesson that when God has something for you, it will be for you. Though in some cases it may tarry, we must remind ourselves during these times that delay is not the same thing as denial. As such, we must hold fast to the exhortation found in Hebrews 6:12, "That ye be not slothful, but followers of them who through faith and patience inherit the promises (KJV)."

Another factor here is to be faithful in the lot that God has appointed you to in the process of waiting. This is what I believed helped me to then obtain my next job. I had now been working at City Hall for a little under a year as a Public Affairs Liaison. Things were very hectic and stressful within the organization I worked for, so much so, that my director had resigned and left me to deal with all of the craziness alone. Despite now being the only one in my department and technically having no real supervision, I decided that I wasn't going to just fly under the radar but instead do my best to make the most out of my current situation. I ended up getting involved with a new school project that one of my fellow colleagues was working on. Although it came with great demands, I felt ready to take on the challenge. What I didn't know at the time is that people were watching me during this process. Because of my role in the project, I was sometimes required to speak at local community meetings, some of which were broadcasted on the local television station.

One day as I was headed up to my office, I saw the Mayor (whose suite was on the same floor) about to get on the elevator as I was getting off. She looked at me and then pulled me aside and said to me, "Young lady I've been watching you and I want you to come work for my office." Initially, I thought she was joking but then a few days later I was summoned to her Business Administrator's Office where I was informed more in detail of how much the Mayor had been impressed with the work she saw me doing in the City. Additionally, she brought up a previous conversation that I had with her during an event several months ago. I had almost forgotten about it but when the Business Administrator mentioned it, I knew exactly what she was referring to.

About seven months prior I was at a City Hall event doing PR duty when I began to engage in a conversation with the Mayor and a local reporter. The Mayor, who was around 81 at the time, was expressing her frustration with how much attention her age carried when there were other issues more pressing, and when it clearly didn't impede her ability to govern effectively. I told her that I agreed and began to share some insight that I discovered using biblical context. She was quite intrigued by this and expressed an interest in hearing more. Later that day or perhaps, the next day I ended up typing a small write up or exegesis on what I was trying to explain—using scripture references to back up my points. I then left it with her secretary and thought nothing more of the matter, at least not until then. Apparently, this act of obedience of really just doing what I felt God wanted me to do ultimately left a lasting an impression on the Mayor, which contributed to her interest in finding out more about me and my accomplishments. Shortly, thereafter, I was offered a position to become her assistant and at the age of 25 became the youngest person on her staff. I would find out later that the Public Affairs position I had previously held was on the verge of getting cut, so God brought me out in the nick of time again and this time with a promotion and raise!

Most recently, the door of employment itself shut in my face as I found myself part of a mass layoff from the City, but just like in every other situation there was purpose. As a result of this occurring several things were able to happen. I was able to start up an organization focused on educating/empowering the unemployed and underemployed, complete the first couple of semesters of a long sought after doctoral program, finish out several online certificate programs, and perhaps my greatest window of opportunity-- embark on my first book writing project. Just think...you may not even be reading this book right now if it weren't for me having this particular door slammed in my face.

## Reflection Point

Have you had any doors closed on you recently? Consider that perhaps God wants to come another way to bring forth your blessing. Sometimes, the ending of one thing really signifies the beginning of something greater. So instead of pouting over your loss, rejoice in the future gain yet to be experienced.

# The Pitfall of Rejection

*The stone which the builders rejected has become the chief corner stone. Psalm 118:22*

It was December 25,1995…as I stared into the mirror with the razor in my hand so many thoughts ran through my mind. Was this the life I wanted to keep living? Did I even matter to anyone? Would anyone miss me if I was gone? As I held the razor to my wrist I contemplated taking my life that day and all over … a gift? The fact is it all started that way but it didn't originate there.

Early that Christmas morning when I awoke with utter excitement to find an abundance of beautifully packaged gifts under the tree, the excitement soon quickly faded away as I combed through them and discovered that only one of the gifts was marked off for me. The rest were designated for my two younger sisters, who at this time were in complete glee as they sat and opened present after present of wonderful surprises. While I would have loved to celebrate with them, I was too busy sulking about how overlooked and abandoned I felt. You see, in my mind I had worked so hard to be a great daughter; consistently making honor roll and never getting into trouble in school (aside from an occasional detention here and there but I digress☺) , so why did I deserve such treatment? (Sidebar: I bet sometimes many of us also feel this way concerning our walk with God.)

To me it all just didn't seem fair. In fact, my whole childhood began to feel like it wasn't fair. So in the mirror that day I stood, staring face to face with an enemy who over the years I've come to know so very well. No matter how much I would try to hide it or suppress it, there it was glaring right back at me, that old familiar face—Rejection!

In fact, my first encounter with it took place at the precious age of 1 when my father an abusive alcoholic abandoned my mother and I, her firstborn. For years since I harbored these feelings of rejection, feelings of nothingness, and deep pockets of emptiness—emotions that always seemed to infiltrate my mind in one way or another and be perpetuated by constant family issues and with the feeling of just not fitting in.

I believe it was these same emotions that drove my cousin to almost take her life in that same place with the same method only several years prior. Thankfully, she was not successful at it and neither was I. No matter how bad I wanted to do it, I simply didn't have the guts to take my life that day and looking back I believe it was just part of God's sovereign plan.

Ultimately, it was nothing short of the grace of God that kept me from pulling the trigger. He had to know that one day my life would carry new meaning. He saw something greater in me that the world around me thought may have never existed. He saw purpose in me. He saw something special waiting to be revealed. He saw someone who, like many before them would have to go through the fire in life only to turn back around and pull someone else out. He Saw Destiny!

He knew, although I didn't realize it at the time, that there was a purpose in me waiting to be fulfilled. Just like there is a purpose my cousin has to fulfill and just like there is a purpose that you, the person reading this book has to fulfill.

I can't help but wonder how many of us experience these negative thoughts and feelings of rejection throughout our lifetime and how often it holds us back. I would imagine that it consumes much more of our time than it should. I'm also willing to bet that it's one of the root causes why many of us never reach our greatest potential in life and fall short of pursuing our purpose and destiny. Just think about it...how many times have you talked yourself out of going after something out of fear of rejection or just not feeling adequate enough? I know that I have countless times, and truth be told I still struggle with it till this day. In fact, this is part of what caused me to sit on this book for seven years! In my mind there was a constant battle as to whether or not I was ready to write a book, whether anyone would want to listen to what I would have to say, and even more what would people think when they saw that how much I really didn't have it all together and that I had skeletons in my closet too.

## People Pleasing vs. God Pleasing

Ultimately, my fear of not wanting to experience those same feelings of rejection as a child caused me as an adult to develop tendencies of... dare I say it... A PEOPLE PLEASER. Yes, there it is, I said it...my name is Keanna and I am a reformed, or shall I say continually being reformed people pleaser. Because truth be told like many struggles in life, there is always the temptation to return back to it but it's at these times I am reminded of Proverbs 26:11 when it says, "As a dog returns to its vomit, so a fool repeats his folly." In no way do I ever want to be likened unto a dog, so I make it a point to press forward and I do so with the revelation and knowledge that the only opinion that truly ever really matters is God's.

Still, this can be easier said than done. I know firsthand, as I've spent countless years of my life trying to please others, keep them happy, and get them to like me; and in the end all I discovered was how insanely impossible it was to accomplish any of the above. Besides this, I also found out how truly unhappy I was as I had begun to lose myself in the process. Often, I would become so caught up in playing the part that I began to forget who I was in the first place. It reminds me of actors and actresses who become so stuck in playing a fictional character that they too lose sight of reality, and in some case their lives because of it. This is no life to live, but many times, it's the life that we choose all because we are afraid of having to deal with that dreaded R word—rejection.

As we all know, the opposite of rejection is acceptance and this is really what many of us crave and desire out of life. Most times, we become people pleasers because we want those around us to accept us, even if they aren't accepting us for the true us and only for the image we represent. In our eyes it's all good because at the end of the day we can say proudly "They Love Us, They Really Love Us." Isn't this what we all want to believe—that we are loved and accepted by all those around us?

Recently, I was reminded about how I had done this in order to be accepted in a previous relationship. The guy who I was dating was very adamant about women dressing in very modest apparel. While I was all for modesty also, his definition turned out to be slightly different from mine. Not only did he frown on anything outside of skirts and dresses, but he also had distaste for anything considered flashy or overly trendy. I can still remember our first date some years ago. At the time, I was still in college and my wardrobe was quite trendy and fun going. I ended up wearing a hot pink hat tilted to the side☺ with the shirt to match and a vintage looking pair of jeans. I was very comfortable with what I had on, but he made it clear that he was not. He informed me that although he had planned to introduce me to his mother that day he decided not to because I looked too flamboyant. (I know what you're probably thinking…why didn't you take the clue and run from the gate? I'm not totally sure but now I can say that this was all for a purpose and he turned out to be a friend if nothing else.)

Afterwards, he went on to tell me that while he felt I was more liberal compared to his more conservative temperament, he felt there was a strong chemistry between us that could not be denied. Suffice it to say, that was the beginning of me getting pulled in; before I knew it I was giving away most of my pants and jeans opting for the more conservative skirts and dresses that he preferred. Although I can't say I went totally off the deep end with it, I still went far enough where I began to lose my own style and to some degree, my sense of identity. Ultimately, it would take several years to regain it all the way back and now having done so, I've resolved to never let it happen again.

I discovered from this that losing one's own identity can be one of the most suppressive and scariest places to be. I use the word scary because many times you don't even realize you lost it until it's gone. In fact, your friends and family will often see it before you get wind of what's really going on. This is why it's not only important to trust your instincts but also trust those that have been placed in your life to help you see what you cannot. Even more, it's important to accept and be happy with whom you are and the skin that God has placed you in. For when you are comfortable with this, you become less prone to embrace anything outside of who you are.

### Good Enough

Good enough…exactly what does this term mean and who is it who decides the barometer by which one is judged on it? For me, it was people—their opinions of me and what they said that seemed to carry so much weight. Next, it was me, perhaps my greatest enemy of all. I was constantly critiquing and beating myself up over even the minutest things.

The fact was that no matter how much I accomplished, I still struggled with believing it was ever good enough—or even more whether I was good enough. I wondered if I was really smart enough, talented enough, thin enough, pretty enough, powerful enough, popular enough…and the list just went on and on. Even if someone had told me otherwise, I would still find it incredibly hard to believe that I was really good enough. As a result, years were spent trying to prove to people and more so to myself, that I was somebody, that I deserved a chance and that it was wrong to be judged based off my very humble beginnings. So I prided myself in excelling in school, being inducted into every honor society you could name…Junior Honor Society, National Honor Society, and finally Phi Beta Kappa Honor Society which can be compared to the ultimate supreme prize in one's collegiate experience. Still, deep down I was always left feeling like somewhere I hand missed the mark—that my good just wasn't good enough. There were thoughts of feeling as if I was much further behind than where I should have been in life and that somehow success (in my viewpoint) had still passed me by.

Quite honestly, it was just up until recently these thoughts persisted to swarm within my mind. Then one day I received a breakthrough. I had just finished an interesting conversation with my good friend Bryant. In this dialogue I proceeded to ask him questions about myself, trying desperately to find answers to that long sought of question of being good enough. Then, as I finally hung up I heard the Lord speak to me ever so softly and say "Keanna, you are good enough…I made you to be good and that's exactly what you are." So simple yet so profound to me: because it carried with it years of hurt and pain. Instantly, tears began to run down my check as I finally got revelation of what the Lord was trying to tell me all along while I was too busy hearing all of the lies—lies from the pit of hell that almost caused me to even abort my dream simply because I thought I wasn't good enough.

On that day it was as if a ton of bricks hit me. No longer did I have to prove myself to anyone for God had already proven it all. So, there I sat as if for the first time it really sank in—I AM GOOD ENOUGH.

Today, I now understand that it was all a trick from the enemy to get me to doubt myself. Just consider the fact…the more he can get us to question ourselves, the less effective we all become in pursuing our purpose and destiny. For this reason, I am totally convinced that having true knowledge and acceptance of who you are and what God has created you to do is one of the most crucial steps on your path to greatness.

If you stand in a similar place today questioning whether or not you are good enough, smart enough, or beautiful enough—the resounding answer to this question is YES! Yes, you are and not just because I said so or because your mom, friend, or significant other said so but simply because God says it. In fact, His word declares that you are fearfully and wonderfully made. You are the apple of His eye. You are uniquely designed, fashioned for success and called to fulfill a purpose that only you can carry out. You see when God created you He had no one else on His mind but you. He wasn't thinking about your neighbor next door or the person He created before you. He had solely you on His mind because He wanted to make sure that like many of His other creations that you would truly be one of a kind. You would be one of His walking masterpieces, indeed, an original design.

# Original Design

*"For we are God's workmanship, created in Christ Jesus to do good works, which God prepared in advance for us to do." -* Ephesians 2:10

I'll never forget some years back listening to a very powerful sermon by T.D. Jakes entitled "Designer's Original." In it he discusses how God uniquely created each and every one of us with a divine purpose in mind. He said that there was things that one person could do that no other, not even their own twin) could do quite like them. Perhaps, this is why we all have certain imprints on us that can also never be carbon copied such as our fingerprints or our DNA. It's amazing to know that out of the billions of people on the planet, there is absolutely no one who shares the same exact fingerprint or DNA as you. This is why they are so useful in identifying individuals. Much of the same can be said of your skills, personality, abilities, experience, and heart—when coupled altogether it will be almost impossible to find anyone who is completely wired the same as you. If you ever had any question about it or doubt, know that for sure you are indeed a rarity, a one of kind.

As I turn my attention back to Bishop Jakes sermon, I have to point out an illustration he used that will always stick with me. He said that if there was a stadium filled of tens of thousands of people and God called your name, no one else could stand up and answer the call but you. Even if they did share the same physical name, the fact of the matter is that God has a personal name that He has for you that distinguishes you from all the rest. This means that only you can answer the call once it goes forth, and only you can walk out the purpose that He placed in you. In the process, know that there are specific people God will place in your path as you go forward and these people will be tailor made for you to reach. In other words, He is looking for you to leave a lasting imprint on someone that only you can make. So why not make it count, right?

Make the decision today to never give up or abort the dream that is within you, for that dream that was divinely inspired by God to go forth just through you. Therefore, you would not only do yourself an injustice, but such the like, you would do God and those who you were called to impact a disservice as well.

Understand that it doesn't matter what you are called to do, but it's the very fact that you, yourself is called to bring it forth which brings all the significance. In this I am reminded of a quote by the late Dr. Martin Luther King: "Everybody can be great, because anybody can serve. You don't have to have a college degree to serve. You don't have to make your subject and verb agree to serve. You only need a heart full of grace. A soul generated by love."

The part you were purposed to fulfill, no matter how great or small is important and adds value to the world. So whatever you do…do your part and don't abort your dream.

### Reflection Point

For the next seven days, I want you to take time out during your day to repeat this declaration until it becomes settled in the inside of you. If necessary, continue the process longer as needed:

"I declare that today I am GOOD ENOUGH. That Jesus Christ died and rose again so that I can be declared the righteousness of God through Christ Jesus. So today I stand on this Word. I renounce every evil spoken, negative word ever pronounced against me and declare that its power is broken from touching my life. I declare that all is well with me—that I am fully accepted and complete in Christ! Therefore, no weapon formed against me will prosper and every tongue that rises against me in judgment shall be condemned. I declare that I am fearfully and wonderfully made, marvelous are your works oh God and my soul knows that full well. I decree that I am the head and not the tail, above and not beneath. I am the apple of my Father's eye and He loves me unconditionally. Nothing can ever separate me from the love of God. Therefore, I will boldly walk out my purpose and will allow nothing to stop me in Jesus name!"

Now may you go forth with no distractions and no hindrances!

# The Dreaded "D" Word...Distractions

*Distractions, distractions everywhere I go, producing only negative reactions as Satan puts on his show.*

*—Excerpt from a Personal Poem*

I have come to recognize distractions as simply a way of life. At some point or another they are going to come, but it's what we do with them that make all the difference. Do we allow them to take us off our course? Or do we buck up against them and give them little to no space in our lives? Years ago I recall having a conversation with an old friend of mine. We were discussing how no matter how effectively we may plan our day, there is almost without fail some form of distraction that tries to interrupt it. Perhaps, you may have experienced some yourself such as when you're in the zone working on a project and suddenly there's a knock at the door, or you're trying to meet a deadline and someone wants to talk your ear off, or my favorite, you're spending time in prayer and then the phone rings, or out of nowhere an ungodly image pops up in your mind. This is the worst! One thing that these all have in common is that they're all great at getting you off focus and typically that is exactly what distractions aim to do. For this reason, my friend would often refer to them as demonic deviations. To put it simply, there are times when the enemy will strategically send detractors our way in an effort to sabotage our plans and get us off track. You see the last thing he wants is for us to be successful in our endeavors, and moreover, leave a positive impact on those around us.

This is why we must always be on guard against the common distractions of life. 2 Corinthians 2:11 instructs us to not be ignorant of Satan's devices...for often the devil is roaming about "like a roaring lion seeking whom he may devour." (1 Peter 5:8) Don't allow him to take you off your course! You can start by applying these four basic principles:

**1. Start Your Day Off Right:** Years ago while taking a creative arts writing course in college, I wrote a short story entitled "The Day I Forgot to Pray." As you would imagine, this story was filled with all kinds of topsy turvy occurrences, obstacles and mishaps. In short, it was completely loaded with DISTRACTIONS! By the way, this is a good time to take note that distractions will often come in different forms of shapes, sizes, and types. Some can even be very unsuspecting or unassuming shall we say. Even something that may seem very innocent such as a co-worker needing to talk with you for a few minutes (at least that's what they may say) about a personal situation they're going through. You being your nice, concerned self goes along with it and puts your already past due project to the side to lend the poor fella or sister an open ear, but little do you know is that what's supposed to be a 5 minute dialogue quickly turns into a 30 minute monologue with no end in sight! What do you do...should you now bring up the fact that you're on a tight deadline and need to get back to work or do you continue to go along with it as you feel your mood quickly go from helpful and concerned to impatient and bothered. Well, the best thing to do is not to get put in this predicament in the first place. Spending time with God early before your day starts helps you to make better decisions with your time because you often come out more focused and more discerning as to the directions life would take you.

**2. Always Have a Plan**: There is a well-known adage that says "If you fail to plan then you plan to fail." How true this statement is! I cannot begin to tell you the countless number of times when I've suffered from not having a valid plan to follow. I'm not just talking about overall long term and short term goals for life though this is a good start, but even more than that we must take daily action steps to fulfill life time goals and this requires a daily agenda for your life.

At times, this could be as a simple as a daily task sheet you write up first thing in the morning and then structure your day around it. For those who tend to be more organized, you may have a daily planner that details what you need to do every hour on the hour. Nowadays, there are so many ways to keep track of our day that you are almost guaranteed to find at least one method that suits you, and when you do be sure to put it to work! For when it comes to this, consistency is the key. Please don't make the countless mistakes I have. In not doing so, I have ultimately lost days and when added up weeks, months, and even years of my life of time wasted as a result of not always following a daily plan or schedule. This is something destiny-minded people simply cannot afford to do.

In one of my favorite books, Commanding Your Morning by Cindy Trimm, a poem called "The Essence of A New Day" pretty much sums up this point:

This is the beginning of a new day
You have been given this day to use as you will.
You can waste it or use it for good.
What you do today is important
Because you are exchanging a day of your life for it.
When tomorrow comes, this day will be gone forever.
In its place is something that you have left behind...

Let it be something good. *–Author Unknown*

So, whatever you do make the best of every day you have because the one thing you can never get back is time.

**3. Submit Your Plan to God**: Proverbs 16:3 instructs us to "Commit to the LORD whatever you do, and your plans will succeed." There is something in being able to take all of our goals, ambitions, and plans and then trustingly hand them over to an All Powerful God, All Seeing God. Truth be told, He could do exceedingly more with our own dreams than we could even imagine or envision within ourselves (Ephesians 3:20). 2 Chronicles 16:9 tells us that God is constantly seeking out opportunities to show Himself strong on our behalf. If this is the case, then God wants to see our plans succeed even more than we ourselves. Still, the key is to make sure they are centered in Him. Whenever they are not centered in God, we are liable to make unwise decisions.

I remember being in my freshman year of college and feeling the pressure of not having lost my virginity. It wasn't that I hadn't had the opportunity to do so, but I was just really particular on who, in my viewpoint would have the honors. Although up to that point I didn't intend to wait until marriage, I still believed it had to be special and it had to be right. What better thing to do, I thought, then to plan it out myself. So plan I did, and since I didn't really have a relationship with God at the time, He was nowhere included in it. Ultimately, I came to the conclusion that the man I was currently in a relationship was not worthy of my prized possession, and so I planned to temporarily break it off with him so that I can then get back with my ex-boyfriend who I felt was more deserving. You see, although we weren't together, we were still good friends and I knew he really cared about me—I just didn't particularly care for some of the unwise decisions he made at times, which is why I also planned to make sure it was just going to be a one-time thing—you know just to break the ice, if you will☺. Then, I would get back with my current boyfriend and continue on with life as usual while creating a memorable first time experience that I could always remember. Makes sense right? Absolutely not! Looking back on it now, I realize it was one of the dumbest plans I could have ever come up with, but at that time, it seemed right to me. Proverbs 14:12 informs us that "There is a way that seems right to a man, but in the end it leads to death." I thank God that He never allowed things to go the way I had planned because in the end I would have only shortchanged myself when God had so much more.

Perhaps, you're in a situation much like that today. Are you holding onto your own plan, when God could have something better for you? I encourage you to take whatever it is and submit it to Him because ultimately He knows what's best for us and He has the power to bring it to pass. So why not trust Him with your dreams!

**4. Stay Your Course**: One of my mentors once told me, "Whatever you do Keanna, do not allow anything to move you off your square." I say the same thing to you today. Once you have established your plans in God, do whatever you have to do to stick with it and don't let anything and I mean anything move you off your square. John 10:10 tells us that the enemy wants to steal, kill, and destroy but Jesus says that He came so that we may have life and have it more abundantly. Once you put your plan into motion understand that there is an all-out assault waged against it; however, the good news is that the power that be with you is greater than anything that can ever come up against you (1 John 4:4).

Make a conscious effort to not be moved by the distractions life may bring your way. This is something I had to do after making a decision to write this book. It seems that once I moved forward in what God told me to do concerning this, everything including the kitchen sink was thrown my way. Out the clear blue sky I all of sudden found myself with no source of income, having to lean on nothing but the sheer grace of God. In the midst of this, my car began to act up and then my mom's car is totaled, and to make matters worse I had to abruptly pull out of my doctoral program that for years I aspired towards completing. It seemed that just when I thought things couldn't get any worse, it took another downward spiral. I'm sure many of you can relate. The interesting thing is that situations like these are not uncommon to those who choose to go after their destiny. Again, the good news is that there is always a light at the end of the tunnel. Our only responsibility is to hold our course and trust God to bring us through.

*God is our refuge and strength, an ever-present help in trouble. Therefore we will not fear, though the earth give way and the mountains fall into the heart of the sea, though its waters roar and foam and the mountains quake with their surging. "Selah"*

*--Psalm 46:1-3*

### Reflection Point

Begin to think about areas in your own life where you feel you're commonly distracted and start putting in place an action plan on how to avert these distractions. Then have someone hold you accountable to it. Keep in mind that sometimes multi-tasking is a distraction in and of itself.

# Overextending One's Self

*"Sometimes we do too much for others that we forget to make ourselves happy. We deem everything and everyone more important than ourselves and think that meeting their needs is more important than meeting our own. But remember if you run out of gas, everyone riding with you will be left stranded too."*
-Bishop T.D. Jakes

What can also be a major distraction in itself is our inability to say "no" or what I would like to call "Being a Savior to the World Syndrome." This especially applies to those who struggle with people pleasing. Typically, individuals like this just want to see everyone happy even if it comes at the expense of their own happiness. As such they will end up overcommitting themselves to things that they have no business getting involved with just to keep the peace or to fulfill what they feel is a personal obligation. I can recall struggling with this for quite some time in my life and even now it still takes a conscious effort to not get sucked in to it.

I remember my college years in particular being the most difficult in this area. To this day I am amazed I was even able to graduate, let alone do so with high honors with all that was going on. I know for a fact that it was nothing short of the grace of God on my life because in the natural it would have appeared that I was way in over my head to do anything but fail. In addition to being a full time student, it was also my responsible to oversee two very active young adult ministries—one on campus and one off campus that served the tri-state area. As a co-founder of both of these ministries, I found myself investing a whole lot of time and effort trying to lay the ground work for a healthy foundation.

In addition to this, I worked part-time and at times up to three jobs at once. I was also active in other extracurricular activities in my school outside of ministry that carried with it its own demands. And finally, what perhaps, seemed to have one of the largest impacts in terms of my focus was my family life.

In order for you to understand what I mean, I believe it's necessary to first give a little background. From the time I moved out of my mom's house at the age of 14 to live with relatives to the time I went off to college, things with my family seemed to take a turn for the worst. At some point, my mom and three siblings were evicted out of their apartment and for a few years stayed with various family members until she was again able to settle back into her own. It was during these years specifically that a paradigm shift had occurred. With me, the oldest, no longer around to help out as much; I believe things eventually began to take its toll on my mom and she got a bit overwhelmed with her situation. For anyone who has ever dealt with the feelings of being overwhelmed, you know that one of the common responses is to simply tune out and I think that's exactly what happened.

Not too long after, I recall having a conversation with my younger sister sometime during my first year or two in college and she shared with my how she felt like mom had begun to become more of a friend than a mom at that point. (A sidebar to any parent reading this book, please understand that one of the worst things you can ever do is dumb down your parenting role with your children to win them over as a friend. Know that it is possible to have a great relationship without going this route and more than anything kids really do desire to have you be exactly what you were designed to be—Parents First. Lord knows there are enough friends out there to go around, but there are very few parents.) Soon after, I listened as this same young sister who I remember only a few years prior as being a bright eyed energetic young girl with pig tails explain to me how she was trying to hide from our family the fact that she was now pregnant at the precious age of 13. From this point on it was an up and down rollercoaster ride with my family. It seemed that every moment I turned around there was some form of emergency—first my baby sister, who is autistic, went missing, then Family Services got involved both with my mom and then with my sister after she birthed my beautiful nephew. In between there were other sorts of emergencies, some of which I may not have full permission to share but I will say this...I believe I was in the hospital's emergency room enough times in the following years for the hospital to mistaken me as one of their own staff members. While some things were major, others were minor but regardless of what it was I always tried to go out of my way to be there.

Eventually, it began to take a drastic toll on me. One day while hugging a friend, he told me that he felt my body trembling. I asked him what he meant and he reiterated that I was shaking, and then went on to compare it to an older and fragile elderly person who was sick except only I was fresh in my twenties and otherwise healthy. I realized later that it was the result of my nerves being affected by all of the recent occurrences in life and as such had now caused this uncontrollable shaking/trembling movement which persisted for some weeks and possibly months as I would recall. Finally, it had reached a point where some of my friends felt the need to intervene. I remember one of my roommates having a very candid conversation with me one day and she said to me: "Keanna, you have to stop trying to be a savior to everyone including your family. There's certain things that only God can do and when you try to act in His stead you only end up hurting yourself and in some cases hindering others." Now, although this may not have been said exactly verbatim, this was exactly what I took away from the conversation that day.

Sometime later when speaking with my friend Joshua, he shared very similar sentiments with me and coupled it with scriptural context that really helped convince me on what I needed to do. He said to me, "Keanna, think about Jesus when He ministered to the people. He didn't stop and attend to the needs of everyone in His path. Even while many may have tried to beckon Him over or try to get his attention, he persisted to remain focused only on what he was called to do. He lived a very purpose driven life that required Him to stay concentrated on the tasks at hand as given by His Father." Suffice it to say, the light had finally began to click on for me and I realized that I was being too busy in other people's matters, whether it was being overinvolved in ministry (which yes can happen), too extended in extracurricular activities, or too consumed with family dilemmas. At the end of the day, I was running myself ragged trying to be all things to all people and found that I was being short changed in the process.

I believe that many perfectionist, people pleasers, and perpetual problem solvers have found themselves in this predicament at one point or another. The tragic part of it all is that getting caught up and spending unnecessary time in various other matters only hinders us from pursuing the things that we are supposed to be doing. I once heard someone put it like this: The moment you say yes to one thing, you inevitably have to say no to another. You simply can't do it all! I must admit, there were times when I became so busy (Being Under Satan's Yoke) in life that I couldn't focus on things like purpose and destiny. These were very foreign to me because I was too focused on just getting through to the next day. This is not God's ideal situation for His children. In fact, peace should be a common thing associated with walking in the will and plans of God. Ergo, anytime you do not have peace or you sense mass confusion, it is time to re-evaluate and possibly re-prioritize your life.

## "No" is an Anointed Word

Over the past few years of my life, I have come to find how truly anointed and powerful the word "no" is. Since I could remember, it was always a common struggle to say "no" to people because I never liked the idea of disappointing them. However, it often had the opposite effect of what was intended because the more I said "yes," the more I overextended myself, and the more it became difficult to follow through with what I initially said I would do. Thus, disappointment became inevitable—only it wasn't just disappointment for them. Ultimately, I would become very displeased with myself for not using better judgment in the first place. Matthew 5:37 tells us that our yes should be yes and our no should be no—nothing more, nothing less. Therefore, it was inexcusable for me to overcommit myself to things and then afterwards have to back out of it because of the lack of feasibility of getting it down. I found that the remedy to this is to place boundaries and limitations from the door and this is why the word "no" is so very important. It not only liberates you but it commands respect by showing others that you have your priorities in line and are not willing for anyone else to come in and control your time, day, and ultimately destiny.

Now, if you're anything like me however, saying no may not always come easy and in order to do so you may have to do some soul searching as to why you find it challenging to use the word "no" in the first place.

Here are some causes I found within myself, and perhaps you could relate to some of them:

**The God Complex**: The first one is perhaps the trickiest and the most subtle because it's rooted in pride and we all know that pride likes to hide, so it can be difficult to trace this one. The God Complex is the tendency within us to what I would like to call "Be Savior to the Whole World." We like to be able to step into any situation and be the solution to it. Someone can be struggling to pay their rent and even though you haven't even paid your own yet and God never told you to intervene, you still feel the need to jump in there and take care of it so you can be "that dude" or "that bosschick". The problem with this is that you risk playing a role you were never intended to play. Also, like I use to often do, you can jump into storms and battles that others simply need to walk through themselves so they can see God pull them through and not you. In order to overcome this you must recognize and accept the fact that it was Jesus who died, and rose again to set people free and not you. As such you need to be sensitive as to how he would have you to move in a person's life-- that's if He would have you to do anything at all. Sometimes, you may find Him telling you to just keep to the side because He needs to use that particular situation to draw that person to Himself. Philippians 2:12 tells us that each individual is called to work out their own salvation with fear and trembling, however, how can they do this if you're always working it out for them?

**The Mother Teresa Complex:** The Mother Teresa Complex is the tendency within us all to just want to help and be there for others. I believe that women are naturally susceptible to this particular complex because God called us to be helpmeets to our husbands and in order to effectively do this we have been wired in this way. As such, we're always looking to just get out there and help people. Unlike the God Complex it doesn't often involve pride but in most cases comes out a sincere heart to want

94

to see people live happier and productive lives. The problem, however, is that in the process of helping everyone we can so often forget to do that which the Lord is requiring of us concerning our own situations. This is something I had to deal with when God first began tugging on my heart to write this book. As I mentioned earlier, the concept for it was given seven years ago but I sat on it, and this was one of the reasons why I did. I had become so accustomed to helping everyone else develop and maintain their own visions, businesses, ministries, etc. that I inevitably neglected mine. Not only was this disrespectful to God because it's like I'm now telling Him that the purpose He placed in me isn't as important as these other things, but it also shortchanges those individuals who are waiting for me to launch out with what God has placed in me. The fact of the matter is that whatever it is that God has placed in you, there are people somewhere in need of it and they are waiting on you, so what are you waiting for?

**The Compensating Complex**: The Compensating Complex is when we may feel as if we are inadequate in certain respects and in order to make up for it we look to receive our value from people. Moreover, we do this by constantly doing things for them, so they can look at us as valuable or needed in their life. The problem with this complex is that all we really are doing to them is making them become co-dependent on us. As a result, they find it difficult to then stand on their own two feet and even more to trust God for the things that they need. The Compensating Complex is nothing more but a trick from the enemy to get us to think that by doing things for others we create a better image of ourselves. However, the truth is that it's when we do things for God which may often involve helping others then our image is solidified. I say solidified because who we are is grounded in Him in the first place and not in what we do.

Ultimately, this complex only provides a cover up of possible esteem issues we have within and these can't be dealt with by simply placing a Band-Aid over it.

**The "I'm Obligated" Complex**: The "I'm Obligated" Complex means exactly what it says. We feel obligated to do things for people because of the weight that they carry in our lives. It may be family, close friends or even those in spiritual authority over us. These are all people who we greatly respect and esteem so the last thing we want to do is say no to them, right? Wrong. When we make the mistake of allowing anyone outside of God dictate what we do at any given time that thing can become idolatry in our lives. In Luke 14: 26 Jesus says, "If anyone comes to me and does not hate his father and mother, his wife and children, his brothers and sisters—yes, even his own life—he cannot be my disciple." Now does this mean Jesus want us to hate those people closest to us? Absolutely not! He is simply using strong verbiage to prove His point and the point of the story is that we must always maintain the proper perspective concerning relationships. In other words, our love and submission to God and His will must be so great that it makes anything else look subpar to it at best. Therefore, we must not let our obsession with being obligated to those around us ever hinder our calling and destiny. Recently while talking to a friend on the phone I shared with him how I'm glad God has finally brought me to the place where I realize my only true obligation outside of following God and His will would be to a spouse and children for ultimately that in itself is part of God's will for your life so in that you are obligated. Anything else you need to always be led by the Spirit of God as to what to get involved with and what not to. If not, you run the risk of possibly being taken advantage of and/or becoming someone's personal puppet. Tell me…are there any strings in your life in need of cutting?

## Reflection Point

Henry David Thoreau once said "It is not enough to be busy. So are the ants." The question is: What are we busy about? I challenge you to take a few minutes to really ponder on this question and then determine if there are any areas in your life that are in need of reprioritization. Make the decision today to not become so consumed in other matters that you forget to consider how much you and the ultimate purpose for your life matters to God.

# Relationship Detours

"…Nevertheless, not my will, but yours, be done."

-Luke 22:42

God's plans and purposes for our lives weigh heavier than anything we can see, including our own will and desires. However, the temptation is to overlook them in turn for what we want and what we see. This can especially be true in relationships. In relationships there is a tendency to believe that at the outset of each, that it is "the one." This desire stems from our will. If you have ever been faced with a situation deemed "do or die" it is by our will that we believe we have to accomplish the task, thus labeling the situation as an "I" had to do what "I" had to do. It is by this same principle; we push relationships to a place WE are comfortable with.

During a recent conversation with my good friend Timothy, he pointed out something I found to be quite interesting. He said to me, "you know I have come to realize that often in life when we keep going in circles with a certain thing (particularly relationships) it's often an indication that there's a clashing of wills—God's will versus our will." Little did he know at the time, he happened to be speaking right into my current situation. Interestingly enough this situation first began 7 years ago not long before the concept of this book was dropped on me. It was around this time I met and developed a relationship with a man I thought for sure was destined to be my husband. I had somehow convinced myself that this was something the Lord intended—I was so convinced that I ultimately ended up sticking around another 7 years waiting for it to come to pass. I use the word "sticking" because it was not always easy holding on to a relationship that in many ways appeared to be a dead end. Still, somehow I managed to view this as part of my true test to see it through and rest on the promises of God. While many of my friends thought I was crazy for this I thought I was simply putting my faith into action. Little did I know the whole time I was being self-deceived so despite it all I STUCK AROUND.

First, I stuck through a year or so of him trying to figure out if he was supposed to be with his ex-girlfriend or with me (this was still during our friendship stage which was also off and on). Although they weren't technically together at the time, in the back of his mind he constantly wondered if God wanted it to be that way. Indeed, his thinking could be compared to what I was experiencing with him. With the exception being the woman he was wondering about was nothing of what one would have imagined for him—meaning she did not share the same spiritual convictions as he did. In short, they were unequally yoked—two people on different paths going in the opposite direction. Interestingly enough some would go on to say something similar about the two of us. While we may have shared some of the same spiritual convictions (i.e. shared the same boat), we differed in many other factors (headed in opposite directions). For instance, he believed that it wasn't ideal for women to hold certain leadership roles in church (pastors, elders, etc.) Suffice it to say, I viewed this much differently, feeling strongly that many women are gifted and called to walk alongside men in the church as God has given many gifts to the entire body (including male and female) for all to benefit.

Joel 2:28-29

*"And afterward, I will pour out my Spirit on all people. Your sons and daughters will prophesy, your old men will dream dreams, your young men will see visions. Even on my servants, both men and women, I will pour out my Spirit in those days.*

To top it all off, I also recognized the call of God on my life to operate in leadership within the body of Christ. Of course this became the topic of discussion between us on numerous occasions. Still, despite these differences I stuck around. Why, you may wonder? Well, for starters, he really was a nice guy and although we didn't exactly see things eye to eye, I saw within him so much potential, and oh how easy it is to fall in love with potential. I also held on too tightly to the possibility of change—a mistake made all too often and one in which I will cover a little more in depth later in this chapter. Ultimately, I got caught up in the belief that perhaps I could change his point of view on some things, but in the end it was me who ended up changing.

Yet, even with all of this some may examine the situation and think this isn't enough to label this relationship as a possible detour. Well, perhaps not, but the following area surely does—INDECISIVENESS. One of the most challenging and frustrating things I had to deal with through the relationship was the 7 years of uncertainty. As much as he would say he wanted for us to get married, he never felt sure that this was what he was actually supposed to do. As such I went through 7 and half years of maybe, perhaps and just not right now all the while trying to convince myself that there was purpose in it if I was just willing to wait it out. Eventually, 2 years became 4 years, which then became 6 years which then I looked up and discovered suddenly I had lost over 7 years of my adulthood life due to his indecision. I would later discover that there was purpose in all of this but marriage wasn't it—at least not between the two of us.

I realize now that if I ever have to wait 7 years for something like this to happen, then there's a good chance it was never meant to be in the first place. While I would have liked to believe that time really could have changed the situation, it simply wasn't true. My waiting for this to happen was no different from staying in an abusive relationship (whether emotional or physical) with the expectation of being able to change them. The reality is only God can change people and even then, we never know when such change will come. In some cases, it may not come until you choose to let that person go whether temporarily or permanently (with the exception of marriage of course in which case you have to stick it out). In other cases He may choose to never change the person but instead choose to change your perspective concerning the situation. In my case, I had to experience both sides of the spectrum. First, the need to let go of the relationship and next, the renewed perspective that came with this. As a result, I was able to get back on track from this detour and in the process become a better person because of it.

*We can make our plans, but the Lord determines our steps. - Proverbs 16:9*

So what happens when after reaching a place of relative comfort we struggle to maintain that comfort, even after confirmation that we are headed in the wrong direction? Fortunately, for those of us who belong to Christ when our plans are contrary to what's best for us, God begins to intervene and determine our steps.

Usually, the reason we struggle to let go even after repeated confirmation is due to pride. Either I struggle to let go of what I have built or I struggle to let go because of all the time that would have become a waste due to my failed effort. I think we can all agree that 7 years is a very long time to have invested in someone. As such, it made it all the more difficult to finally break things off when it was time, but then The Lord gave me revelation of the following: **Sometimes God doesn't give you what you think you want, not because you don't deserve it but because you deserve so much more**. I realized then that if I didn't let go I could potentially lose out on the best God had waiting for me.

In other words, I had to reach a point of understanding that my will wasn't best for me, and then accept the fact that God had something else in mind that at the time I could not see. When we get to this place where our desire truly becomes to please God, we past our feelings of my will be done to truly meaning "thy will be done" (Matthew 6:10).

## Breaking the Feel Barrier

1 Peter 1:24-25

*"People are like grass, their beauty is like a flower in the field. The grass withers and the flower fades. But the word of the Lord remains forever."*

People will come and go but often, I have made the mistake of letting go of people perhaps I should have held onto and holding onto people I should have let go of. Why? …Emotion.

Webster's second definition of emotion is a state of feeling. Feelings seek to override the mental state of reason. Through many of life's experiences we are trained to react based on emotions; from relationships to shopping. However, reacting based on emotion undermines our God given intellect which was given that we may have Dominion over our emotions.

In my experience, allowing my emotions to have control has often led to a place of dim spiritual light. It causes us to see things through our emotional eyes which tend to focus mainly on situational outcomes based on how we would feel. Ultimately, this only leads us to more pain as opposed to avoiding it, but fortunately God does not allow us to stay there too long. For more often than not, the painful route is usually the route God calls us out. We just have to be willing to take heed. This is where the word of God becomes even more vital.

God's word will always have something to say on our situations, however, we can potentially miss it when we are focused too much on how "we" feel. Moreover, we must recognize that our feelings may come and go, but the word of the Lord stands FOREVER. Don't ignore His word! Unlike your feelings, it is not fickle or erratic but will be standing long after the emotions have subsided.

### Understanding His Will Even When I Don't Understand

Isaiah 55:4
"For just as the heavens are higher than the earth, so my ways are higher than your ways and my thoughts higher than your thoughts."

How much do you trust God with your life? Enough to allow Him to choose the perfect season...perfect person...perfect process...perfect job? The fact of the matter is God has a purpose for our lives—a very specific one directly related to the experiences He has allowed us to experience. **The mate He has for you also serves those exact purposes, in other words, the will fits His purpose perfectly.** So, what happens if you don't understand them? Obviously, if they were understood clearly at the outset we would line our purpose up perfectly, choose the right mate and move right along with His will. However, we are not meant to know all there is to know at once! But this is what we do need to know:

Romans 8:28

*And we know that God causes EVERYTHING to work together for the good of those who love God and are called according to His purpose for them.*

(By the way, if you are looking for proof that you are called, just check out the rest of the book you are reading☺.)

So even if you find yourself in a place where you don't understand, know and remember that what you are experiencing will work for your good. Trust Him enough to walk away, stay, or not proceed in the first place. Most importantly trust His will.

Detours, detours, detours…we learn from the scripture above that they all serve purpose. This means that even our own "self-inflicted" detours can and will be used for our good. Even our deepest sin can be used to serve God's ultimate purpose. God has all things serve His plans and He will deliver you to the place He wants you when the time is right.

So what happens once you have been delivered…?

When God has undeniably delivered you to the place He wants you, it's not the time to sit back and place things on cruise control. There is a trap that lies in wait for all of us in our human frailty—the U-turn. The U-turn is the tragic place in relationships (be it relationship to lifestyle, addiction, or people) where we choose to forget what God has done and remember "the good" of the wayward path.

James 1:23-24

"For if you listen to the word and don't obey, it is like glancing at your face in a mirror. You see yourself, walk away, and forget what you look like."

In relationships with people a U-turn usually comes in the form of a reaching from the one who was left to the one who is leaving in an attempt to  break the made up mind of the one who has decided there is something better. As soon as that made up mind cracks, the U-turn has begun. U-turns can vary in lengths and range in time periods. For me, my U-turn may have turned more into an overlapping circle because that's how many times my ex and I went back and forth in our relationship. For others, U-turn can turn into an entire lifetime of willfully going in the wrong direction. The greatest danger in a U-turn is that the further you travel from the truth after tasting the wonderful path God has for you, the more hardened your heart becomes, thus the more force (pain) God has to use to bring you to a place of broken repentance.

John 10:29

"My Father, who has given them to me, is greater than all; no one can snatch them out of my Father's hand." (NIV)

Fortunately, with God there is always good news! Part of the good news for us is that regardless of where we are (be it far along the U-turn or not), we will not be plucked from His hand. Pain is a useful tool to turn us from our evil, and our loving Father in His infinite wisdom will not hesitate to use it to spur us back towards our destiny.

If today, you find yourself in a place where you have strayed from the path to your destiny…Cry Out! He will help reset your course. If you are having your made up mind attacked…Cry Out! He has the power to keep your mind. If you are the invader of a made up mind…Stop! That person has things to do and places to go! There is danger in opposing God's will, and besides, He has greater purpose for you than you can ever imagine!

Things You Need to Know While Moving Forward…

In a relationship, especially one designed for marriage, it's essential that the two are on the same path and page. To start off both should share the same convictions and should also have common interests and passions. Next, there must be a strong foundation of trust. This becomes particularly important during tough and challenging times. Keep in mind that trust and love go hand and hand for usually it's the love you have for someone which then enables you to trust them openly and freely. Thus, love and trust are essential. When it comes to marriage, it is important that both are anchored in God first. If not, then one can make the mistake of allowing failed high expectations cause possible rifts in the relationship. To put it simply, as a woman I may look to my husband to provide and protect, but I should do it with the expectation that he is likewise looking to God to be the ultimate sustainer and will make the provision necessary for him to play the role he was designed to be and vice versa. As such, the pressure again is placed back on God where it belongs, and we are in essence trusting God for our spouse's abilities to meet certain needs.

Additionally, remember that God will never go against His word, so nor should you. Even though God uses our sin for His greater good, we should never willfully walk into a relationship contrary to God's word. You must also understand that God has great plans for you that are far better than you can imagine. Don't hold on to what He has asked you to let go. He only asked you for it, so He could give you something better.

2 Corinthians 5:17 (KJV)

*"Therefore if any man be in Christ, he is a new creature: old things are passed away; behold, all things are become new."*

We all fall short of God's glorious standards; remember that about those who have hurt you. You are becoming new; the past scars of abuse, mistreatment, and degradation are passed away. They have no bearing on your future. Even more, Isaiah 61:3 tells us that "to all who mourn in Israel, he will give a crown of beauty for ashes, a joyous blessing instead of mourning, festive praise instead of despair. In their righteousness, they will be like great oaks that the LORD has planted for his own glory." It is important that you remember this as you move forward as it can make the difference of you growing bitter or growing better.

## Reflection Point

Relationships can be a very tricky, especially when we decide to take them into our own hands and deem what we believe to be best for ourselves. During a recent vacation, I met and conversed with a nice older couple. At first glance they appeared very happy together, but then as I begin to talk more with the gentleman aside from his lady, I would soon discover that he wasn't happy at all. In fact, he went on to share with me how unhealthy their relationship was for him and how it only seemed to pull him down and further away from God. He said that it had caused him to drink more and do other things he should not be doing. For a moment he felt like his entire relationship with God was in jeopardy because of this situation, but then I began to explain how loving and forgiving God is and how there is always the ability to turn things around. That day he made the decision that he was going to break things off with his girlfriend and refocus in on God. He was pretty adamant about it feeling strongly that he no longer wanted it to hinder his ability to move forward.

Is there a relationship or relationships in your life that his hindering your ability to progress? If so, encourage you to follow in the steps of this man and choose today to sever it because in the end, it will only do more harm than good. Like him, you have to make up in your mind that it's no longer worth sacrificing lasting happiness and fulfillment for temporal and fleeting feelings of pleasure. Don't settle, instead wait on the best God has for you.

## Not All Detours Are Created Equal

*"A journey is like marriage. The certain way to be wrong is to think you can control it."*- John Steinback

## Learning the Lesson

While it's true that there is purpose in all things God allows, there are some detours we may find ourselves in a little longer because of an issue within that God is trying to work out of us. The fact of the matter is that things such as our own self-pride, stubbornness, disobedience, etc. can cause us to have to spend a little more time in just so God can work in out of us. An example mentioned earlier in the book is the one concerning the children of Israel who wondered in the wilderness for 40 years on a journey that should have only taken 2 weeks. However, this had to be done so that God could deal with their complaining, ungrateful attitude. Like many of us, they just weren't prepared to walk into God's promises because they weren't yet in a place where they could handle it. You see, God in all of His perfection understands the unique frailties of human beings. He knows when we're ready for something and when we're not ready. So that we don't mess up or abuse the gift/promise He has for us, He goes through great lengths to ensure that we are in fact prepared for it before it comes.

I can remember for years thinking that I was ready for marriage. In my eyes, I thought that I had all of the necessities packed down. I had obtained my Master's degree by age 23, purchased my first home at age 25 and in the same year landed a great job working for the mayor of the town I grew up in! I just knew I had my stuff together and so for the life of me couldn't understand why God had not seen fit for marriage to come in the picture. Then a few years later while praying for God to send the right spouse to me, God in turn, asked me if I was prepared to be the right spouse. In other words, He wanted me to become the wonderful loving spouse (or in my case wife) I hoped my husband would one day be to me. I guess you could say that this is when the harsh reality that I still had a long way to go came tumbling down upon me. I realized that I needed to change. Even more, I realized that for this to happen, I would need to do a lot of soul searching, a lot of purging and a lot of dying to self. Through this, God helped me to understand that being prepared for marriage is less about having a nice job with a good 401(k) plan and more about having the right heart to receive the blessing God would one day bring to me. It's about truly understanding the purpose of marriage, and moreover, my purpose as a helpmeet to my spouse. Not having this revelation will make one ill prepared to step into that next season in their life no matter how much they think they are ready.

In fact, the same can be said of any season life would bring whether it's stepping into a new career, ministry, writing a book, etc. If we don't take the time to properly prepare for it, then we only hinder and delay the process coming forward into our lives. Moreover, what better time to prepare then while in a detour? Let's face it, these are the times when the kinks are supposed to be ironed out; tough lessons are learned, and great revelation is brought forth thus changing your life for the better and making you more equipped for your destiny.

# Gaining New Perspective

This past summer, my family and I decided to take a vacation to South Carolina. Though I sometimes dread taking this 11 hour drive, I always find that it's worth it due to the beautiful sights and pristine ocean views. As usual, I took on the challenge of driving the entire trip there, but this particular time I did so after having only a few hours of sleep. Suffice it to say, I started feeling the tug of sleep on me about 8 hours into the trip and the fact that everyone else had seemingly dozed off into la la land didn't help, nor did the fact that I had just eaten (some of you know what I mean by this☺).

So there I was desperately trying to fight back the strong grip of sleep. Though I had successfully averted a couple of close calls, it now got to the point where I realized I couldn't take that risk anymore. For it was becoming more and more difficult for me to maintain my focus on the road as my eye lids began to feel like 2 ton bulldozers. Finally, in desperation I woke my mom out of her sleep and asked if she could take over for a little while so I could push past the sleepiness. As she slowly began to regain awareness, I proceeded to share with her that my intentions was to pull over on the shoulder so that we can make a quick transition and stay on schedule. However, she took note of an upcoming exit sign and suggested it would be better to just take that and play it on the safe side. Despite my uneasiness and immediate hesitation, I went ahead and took it just not wanting to prolong the dialogue as my tiredness began to reach the point of unbearable. So against my better judgment, I forced the turn off onto the exit and thus began the start of our hour long detour!

Immediately upon pulling off we realized that the exit was really just an entrance to another highway—one in which took us way off course. Since it was no way to back up or hit the reverse button we had to just ride it out. Ultimately, we had to drive about 8 to 10 miles before seeing another exit sign which we immediately took only to find it led us to yet another....you guessed it—highway! At this point I had managed to break through my sleepiness. I believe it was a combination of shock mixed with frustration along with a determination to get us back on the correct route and try feverishly to make up the wasted time.

After the second half of the detour, I decided it would be best to pull over and get some gas, and I'm glad we did for it was timely indeed. Not only did it allow for a short break from hours of driving but it also allotted me the time to gain a better perspective of the current situation. Truth be told, up to this point, I was doing some serious pouting. I found myself so dismayed by the whole ordeal that I could barely bring myself to focus on anything good about what had taken place, but then the Lord gave me a better understanding.

He proceeded to show me that sometimes in life we will make the mistake of taking the wrong path, but what we are able to gain from it can make all the difference. For instance, through this situation the Lord was able to show me how easy it is to misjudge and make poor decisions when we are not focused and alert. My tiredness had caused me to not be fully aware and cognizant of my surroundings and where I was heading. Looking back on that rash decision to steer off on the wrong exit, I realize that if I had been better rested and prepared, I probably would have seen it coming and recognized in advance that it was a road I needed to avoid. Moreover, I believe 1 Peter 5:8 further puts it in perspective as it tells us to be "sober and vigilant" understanding that we are up against a very formidable opponent.

The interesting part is that I was not alone in my error. My mom, being somewhat out of it herself was not necessarily the voice of wisdom at that point. Understand that there will be times when you also have to be mindful of the counsel you receive from others, especially if you perceive that they aren't necessarily in the best position to be giving advice. You can say it was like the blind leading the blind because neither one of us could have imagined the consequences to a bad decision made in haste. Much of the same can be said of life when we unknowingly or through ill advice go about pursuits, endeavors, relationships, and courses of life without having the correct insight and understanding of what we are really getting ourselves into.

## Light at the End of the Tunnel

Nonetheless, when we do find ourselves in such predicaments—and it's almost inevitable we all will, it's important to remember that it's not the end of the world. I repeat, IT IS NOT THE END OF THE WORLD! Sometimes, it's important that you remind yourself of this. Although you may feel like all is lost, it really is not. In fact, for a few minutes I felt this way after the unexpected detour in our trip. While someone else may look at it and say it wasn't a big deal. In my mind at the time, I was completely devastated. Now, however, I can look back at it and say it really wasn't that serious even though I may have not felt that way at the time. You see, often, when you are in the midst of going through a situation it can feel as if a 100 pound weight has been added to it. It can make a sunny, beautiful day all of sudden feel dark, gloomy and gray. Sometimes, we'll even beat ourselves up over it, angry that somehow we missed the mark and sad that now there are consequences to be dealt with. Still, I'm here to encourage you that it doesn't have to always feel this way, but instead if we're willing to look for it we will often find light at the end of the tunnel.

Moreover, in order for us to experience this quick turn-around, we must be willing to follow a few steps. For me, the first step was choosing to not harbor on the downsides and instead gain a more positive perspective. In order to effectively do this, I had to stop, take a step back and regroup. Pulling over at the gas station was just the break I needed to physically, emotionally, and spiritually get myself back on track. I stopped driving, cleared my mind and gave the situation over to God trusting that He had it all under control. This is the approach one should take with the setbacks experienced in life.

We must be willing to take our hands off the wheel (or off our own will should I say). This must take place not only physically but mentally as well. I can't tell you the numerous times I have so called let something go when in my mind I was still attached to it and holding on for dear life. It reminds me of the story with the young child who was asked to hand over their beloved toy to his father, and as he did he still had his two little hands gripped tightly on the other end of it so that it was never really released. Eventually, the dad has to literally pry it out of his hands. I wonder how often God has to do this with us? How many times has He had to force His hand to remove something toxic from our lives, whether it is a bad relationship, job, or an unhealthy attachment to something? Although this is a common scenario played out time and time again, the truth is that it doesn't have to be. It goes back to the whole concept of "by force or by choice." This means we can easily avoid some of the pain associated with forced detachments if we exercised more of a willingness to participate in the removal process. It's similar to having a tooth removed; the more you try to buck up against it by moving and wiggling around you only prolong the process and make it even more painful. So why not simply relent, and go along with it? It's like what God said to Saul in Acts 26:14, "It is useless for you to fight against my will (NLV)." In the end, we really only hurt ourselves. Besides, as the popular phrase goes on Star Trek, "Resistance is futile."

Even more, I have come to the realization that one of the greatest places of liberty is in knowing that things are in God's hands. It's in not having control of the reigns we are accustomed to holding on so tightly. It's in the beauty of letting go and letting God. Until we are able to get to this place, we'll never be able to experience true rest in Him, true peace that transcends, or true love that remains and supersedes whatever we may be going through at any given time. Moreover, I believe this is part of what Jesus had in mind when he quoted Matthew 11 verses 28 and 29:

*"Come to me, all you who are weary and burdened, and I will give you rest. Take my yoke upon you and learn from me, for I am gentle and humble in heart, and you will find rest for your souls."* (NIV)

Getting to this place allows God the opportunity to take over our situation completely as if it were His very own and when He does, there's no telling what He is able to do.

In my case, God was able to bring forth to me a renewed perspective along with strength and stamina to keep pushing. While in the beginning I wanted to give up and just have my mom do the remaining of the driving, with Him in the driver seat that no longer became a necessity or even an option. For there was a fresh spark in me that said you can do this, you can finish this out strong and by His grace that is exactly what happened! It may have taken nearly 12 hours that day but we finally made it

115

to our destination and I'm happy to say I finished what I started but I didn't do it alone—I did it having God with me every step of the way. Likewise, God wants to be beside you too as you complete your own journey. Yes, the road may get bumpy at times and you may experience frustrating moments, however, in making the conscious effort to give control over to Him you'll soon find more than enough strength to see you through.

In this I'm reminded of a quote coined by Don Williams Jr. which says, "The road of life twists and turns and no two directions are ever the same. Yet our lessons come from the journey, and not the destination." Ultimately, God allowed me to gain an appreciation of the detour that came our way. Because just like many detours in our lives—whether good, bad, or indifferent they have a tendency to show us how strong we really are. Not only does it test our ability to handle challenging circumstances, but it also gives us an opportunity to establish where our trust really lies. In other words, do we depend on ourselves to get through the trials and set-backs in life or is our dependency on God—where it really should be?

Perhaps, the answer to that question for you lies in your next detour…and if you just keep on living you may discover that it is just around the corner. When it does come your way, remember to keep in mind a few important things:

1.  God is in control! Nothing happens without His permission, knowledge, or orchestration.

2.  He wants the best for you! He absolutely wants the absolute best for you and that best is Him!

3.  He knows better than you! God can see all of time all at once, therefore, He can see the results even when we can't.

It's obvious that we can only see that which we have already experienced. Conversely, God can see everything that has EVER been experienced or that EVER will be! Therefore, know that He is in control, wants the best for you, and that He knows what's best, so why not trust Him?

Moreover, also know that trials don't last always! At some point they will have served their purpose. It will end, and there will be something new that has occurred; and possibly something new that has been birthed. That time comes when we learn the lesson; when we let God have His way. Remember, the sooner...the better. The sooner you learn the route, the sooner you no longer get lost. In order words, it pays to be a fast learner, so Learn FAST!

## Reflection Point

*"Experience is a hard teacher because she gives the test first, the lesson afterwards."*                                   - Vernon Saunders Law

The reality is that some of the greatest lessons learned in life are often taught through experience. Although we may not always understand it at the time, if we play close attention we'll soon find that even in what appears to be the worst situations in life can hold within it some of the most precious gems of life—lessons learned.

Take the time to recall at least three personal lessons you were able to learn through a trial, detour, or challenging circumstance. Then reflect on how learning these lessons have benefited your life whether through growth, revelation, or the ability to use it to bless someone else.

# The Paradigm Shift

*"When you change the way you look at things, the things you look at change" –Wayne Dyer*

There are times when I still reflect back on the day I was notified that I was one of over one hundred people to be laid off in the beginning of 2011. I had very mixed feelings on that day. On the one hand, I knew this would end (at least temporarily) a life of financial comfort that I was experiencing for some years. It's so easy to get used to that steady stream of income when you know for certain that the check comes every two weeks or for others, every week. However, this was all about to change for me. I knew that what perhaps was my greatest security blanket was suddenly being violently torn away from me, but most importantly I knew that life as I knew it would never be the same. I ended up being right on both but what I couldn't see immediately was just how all of this was going to work out in my favor.

Nothing could have prepared me for the some of the financial struggles that I experienced during the next year and half; but at the same time, no one could have fully convinced me of all the victories that it would bring in the process. While I was confident that God had me and would keep me through it all, to then actually see Him do it was still pretty much mind blowing. Without me even realizing it, God single-handedly used this situation to help propel me full throttle into my destiny. Through this one event, so began the beginning of a divine paradigm shift in my favor.

Some may wonder what I mean when I use the terminology "paradigm shift". According to the World English Dictionary, a paradigm shift is "a fundamental change in approach or assumptions." It was initially coined by U.S. philosopher T.S. Kuhn in 1962 when he wrote The Structure of Scientific Revolution. In this theory, Kuhn argues that "scientific advancement is not evolutionary," but rather is a "series of peaceful interludes punctuated by intellectually violent revolutions", and in those revolutions "one conceptual world view is replaced by another". In other words, "think of a paradigm shift as a change from one way of thinking to another. It's a revolution, a transformation, a sort of metamorphosis. It just does not happen, but rather it is driven by agents of change."

Change when used in this way can sometimes come off a little frightening. It often requires us to not only begin thinking differently in our lives but also doing differently. In other words, there are new requirements and/or demands placed on us with the expectation that we will shift as necessary in order to be transformed in our way of thinking and way of doing. Often times, this requires us to move beyond our comfort zone and/or place of security that we have easily latched on to. This place can look differently for each of us. Our area of comfort can be in our job, relationships, possessions, way of thinking, etc. It is simply an area in which we have been used to and accustomed with to the point where any change in this area can cause immediate ruffles. Interestingly enough this is exactly the kind of place God will often have us in when he does some of the greatest work in our lives. The key for us is being able to see it for all that it's worth—the ability to transform us.

## Being Transformed for Purpose

*Do not conform any longer to the pattern of this world, but be transformed by the renewing of your mind. Then you will be able to test and approve what God's will is—his good, pleasing, and perfect will.* Romans 12:2 (NIV)

Anyone familiar with the process of a butterfly understands that it is exactly that—a process. It doesn't simply wake up one night and miraculously go from being a caterpillar to a beautiful butterfly. The process begins with the caterpillar building a cocoon around itself, which is called a pupa. Not only does this covering operate as an incubator but it also helps protect the caterpillar during this delicate developmental stage. As an aside, protecting yourself is critical as you are being prepared for your destiny. You have to look at it as if you are literally pregnant with a baby because you are impregnated with something. Women who are pregnant usually don't surround themselves with just anyone nor do they go just anywhere. They are very protective about the seed that they are carrying and thus are mindful of the environment it is exposed to. In addition to this, pregnant women are also instructed to not take in other possible influencers such as alcohol, drugs, or even certain vitamins due to any possible adverse effects it could have on the baby they're carrying.

So I ask how much more of the same for you as you are impregnated with and carrying seeds of purpose and destiny within you? You have to make it a priority to protect it at all costs. This may mean disassociating yourself from negative people or those who seem content on just settling for status quo. Moreover, you must understand that what you surround yourself with ultimately plays a huge role in your ability or inability to pursue destiny. There is a popular adage which says you can only go as high as the people you surround yourself with, so if every time you look around you see only pessimistic people who have given up on their dreams and succumbed to the everyday rat race in life, then this too is what you can look forward to.

121

Whether we like it or not, the company we keep places an integral role in our overall development and achievements in life. 1 Corinthians 15:33 tells us "Do not be misled: 'Bad company corrupts good character.'" The people we are surrounded by will almost always have some kind of influence on us—whether good or bad. **So if you had to choose from being alone or being in bad company, choose being alone because at least then you know if you fail, you have no one to blame but yourself.**

The next stage in the butterfly transformation process is known as the metamorphosis stage. This stage is where most of the change tends to occur. Although on the outside it would appear that the caterpillar is at rest, he is very much at work. Part of this work involves him partially dying off. He does this by digesting itself from the inside out, and then salvaging some of its old tissues to help create his new body. This process reminds me of the scripture found in Ephesians 4:22-24 where it says, "You were taught, with regard to your former way of life, to put off your old self, which is being corrupted by its deceitful desires; to be made new in the attitude of your minds; and to put on the new self, created to be like God in true righteousness and holiness." No process can involve true transformation without the dying off of something because often you will have to get rid of some of the old to make room for the new that comes along with the transformation. Again this involves change and the willingness to no longer be stuck in the same way of thinking and/or doing things.

*"And no one pours new wine into old wineskins. If he does, the wine will burst the skins, and both the wine and the wineskins will be ruined. No, he pours new wine into new wineskins."*-Mark 2:22

The last stage in this process involves the actual emergence of the beautiful butterfly. Keep in mind that this part is no cake walk either because typically, in order to break out of the shell, the butterfly has to push and struggle in order to make it out. The beauty however, is that in this struggle the butterfly's wings are strengthened and developed thus enabling him to fly and soar. Without this, it is likely the butterfly would not make it much longer after its appearance. I think this is why you hear so many stories of people who have reached a certain plateau of success or fame only to then fall flat on their face. How? Simply because they missed this last step. Somehow they were able to go straight to their target without developing the qualities and attributes to keep them there. Don't let this be you. Take the time to go through the process and learn everything God is trying to teach you through each detour and challenge. Even when you can't quite make it out, ask Him for the wisdom to show you and make it clear so that you get everything He has for you through the experience. Believe me; He wants nothing hidden from you, so just ask.

*"Ask and it will be given to you; seek and you will find; knock and the door will be opened to you."*- Matthew 7:7

## Let There Be Light

*"Your word is a lamp to my feet and a light to my path."*
*–Psalm 119:105 (NJKV)*

I believe all of us occasionally have what I would call an "Aha!" moment when the light bulb goes off and all of a sudden we see things more clearly than we did before. Many times, this is what is needed to get us on the right track concerning our future direction and path that we choose.

One day while having a conversation with my Aunt Pat, she shared with me something that I will never forget. She said,

"You know what Keanna, sometimes we may find ourselves at places in life where we lack clarity and direction for the next step to take and I believe it's at these times that we need to declare boldly out of our mouths "Let there be light." This means let there be clear illumination on my path, so I can not only see where I am currently, but also visualize where I am going or need to go.

Four simple words they are, yet they carry with them so much power and potential. Just think about it; it was these same four words that in Genesis 1:3 took a dark and void place and instantly turned it into a well-lighted canvas that we now all earth. Simply amazing, wouldn't you say?

Interestingly enough light is also symbolic of Jesus. In John 8:12, Jesus said, "I am the light of the world. He who follows me shall not walk in darkness, but have the light of life."

This means that whenever you declare "Let There Be Light", you are asking for Jesus, Himself, to come up into your situation. And when He does all darkness has to go, for light and darkness cannot coexist.

### Reflection Point

Many times in life, it all comes down to how we see things. Either we see the cup as half empty or as half full, for ultimately it's our perspective on a situation which then causes us to respond a certain way. So much truth there is in the statement: "Perception becomes reality." Therefore, it is important that you take steps to ensure that your outlook on life is a positive as possible no matter what trouble it brings. In this, I am reminded of an excerpt from a book entitled "Tough Times Never Last, But Tough People Do" by Robert H. Schuller:

"Every problem, even yours, is loaded with possibilities. You can turn your mountain into a gold mine. Try "possibilitizing." Believe that every time one door closes, another will open. Sublimate your problem. That means believing that every adversity holds within it the seeds of an undeveloped possibility. God uses life's bruises! When you can't eliminate the problem; sublimate it. Turn the stumbling block into a stepping stone."

# The Detour Is the Path

*"A truly happy person is one who can enjoy the scenery while on a detour." -Anonymous*

A common phrase often quoted by one of my pastors, Isha Edmondson, says that nothing happens just by happenstance. Or as many of you may have heard it put before, *everything happens for a reason*. There is so much truth to be found in both of these statements. However, often times when we are going through the tough seasons in life it can be difficult seeing the purpose behind it. Nonetheless, it doesn't mean it's not there. It's no different from the wind or the air we breathe. Just because we aren't able to see it, doesn't mean it fails to exist. The reality is that there is purpose in every situation we go through in life--the good, the bad, and the ugly. I know that it may be hard to comprehend at times but even painful experiences such as abuse, rejection, and loss can be used as part of God's perfect plan. In fact, Genesis 50:20 tells that even the very things that may have been meant for our evil, God will use for our good. "

You see, God has an ultimate plan behind everything we face in life. Although we may not always see it or understand it, He always has a reason behind what He allows us to go through. For this reason, I have come to refer to Him as the Master Strategist. There are things that God does that I could never fathom to come up with or plan, but somehow He does it and all the while knowing that it's going to accomplish an ultimate plan. Consider this story entitled "Jesus in my Heart," for example:

Tomorrow morning," the surgeon began, "I'll open up your heart..." "You'll find Jesus there," the boy interrupted.

The surgeon looked up, annoyed. "I'll cut your heart open," he continued, "to see how much damage has been done..." "But when you open up my heart, you'll find Jesus in there."

The surgeon looked to the parents, who sat quietly. "When I see how much damage has been done, I'll sew your heart and chest back up and I'll plan what to do next."

"But you'll find Jesus in my heart. The Bible says He lives there. The hymns all say He lives there. You'll find Him in my heart."

The surgeon had had enough. "I'll tell you what I'll find in your heart. I'll find damaged muscle, low blood supply, and weakened vessels. And I'll find out if I can make you well."

"You'll find Jesus there too. He lives there."

The surgeon left. The surgeon sat in his office, recording his notes from the surgery, "...damaged aorta, damaged pulmonary vein, wide-spread muscle degeneration. No hope for transplant, no hope for cure. Therapy: painkillers and bed-rest. Prognosis: "here he paused, "death within one year." He stopped the recorder, but there was more to be said. "Why?" he asked aloud. "Why did You do this? You've put him here; You've put him in this pain; and You've cursed him to an early death. Why?"

The Lord answered and said, "The boy, My lamb, was not meant for your flock for long, for he is a part of My flock, and will forever be. Here, in My flock, he will feel no pain, and will be comforted as you cannot imagine. His parents will one day join him here, and they will know peace, and My flock will continue to grow."

The surgeon's tears were hot, but his anger was hotter. "You created that boy, and You created that heart. He'll be dead in months. Why?"

128

The Lord answered, "The boy, My lamb, shall return to My flock, for he has done his duty: I did not put My lamb with your flock to lose him, but to retrieve another lost lamb."

The surgeon wept. The surgeon sat beside the boy's bed; the boy's parents sat across from him.

The boy awoke and whispered, "Did you cut open my heart?" "Yes," said the surgeon. "What did you find?" asked the boy. "I found Jesus there," said the surgeon. *–Author Unknown*

Romans 8:28 tells us that all things, not just some things, and not just the good things but that ALL things work together for the good of those who love Him, who have been called according to His purpose. The important part is that you have to know that God loves you and thus has nothing but the best intentions for you despite what things may look like. Second, you have to know that you have been designated by Him to fulfill a specific purpose. That's right you have been called— singled out by name to do something that only you can do. Bearing this in mind makes it easier to understand exactly how God intends to use every detour/obstacle to serve a purpose in your life. Remember, this even includes our own "self-inflicted" detours. Yes, he can and will often even use these for our good.

Jeremiah 29:11

*"For I know the thoughts that I think toward you, said the LORD, thoughts of peace, and not of evil, to give you an expected end."*

Many of us have heard this verse spoken numerous times but how often do we really stop to consider and reflect on its meaning. The fact of the matter is God really does have an expected end for you. Where you currently are in your life at this moment in time is by no means the end all to be all for you. God has so much more. In fact, He hand-picked you for destiny; He placed things (gifts, talents, dreams, visions) in you like no one else so that you could accomplish things that no one else can accomplish.

The key is to not get comfortable where you are, nor should you be discouraged. Walk forward in your purpose "being confident of this, that he who began a good work in you will carry it on to completion until the day of Christ Jesus." Phil 1:6 (NIV).

### Allowing God Ordained Interruptions

In today's busy society, one of the things that can sometimes bother us the most is to be interrupted from our daily routine and schedule. However, we must still be open to these, particularly when it's divinely inspired. The fact is that there are going to be times in life where we must be willing to allow for such detours and interruptions knowing that God has designated a specific purpose behind it. In this, I am reminded of a few stories found in the Bible.

Peter and Paul - In Acts 3:3-8 we see an account of a story where Paul and Peter were on their way to the temple (or shall we say church) and while on the way there they were interrupted by a crippled man who proceeded to ask them for money. Their response to this man was "Silver or gold I do not have, but what I have I give you. In the name of Jesus Christ of Nazareth, walk." (v.6) Peter and Paul then proceeded to help this man up as for the first time in his life he was able to walk! Absolutely filled to brim with joy this once crippled man began to leap and jump shouting for joy as he praised God. What makes this story even more amazing is that as a result of this, Peter and Paul was given a platform to proclaim the gospel to a group of people who may have never been open or receptive to hear if it weren't for

130

this miracle taking place. Could you imagine what would have happened if they simply ignored the crippled man?

Phillip and the Ethiopian (Acts 8) - As the passage tells us, the Ethiopian that Phillip later witnessed to was nowhere on his agenda for that day. In fact, neither was his journey to Gaza. Phillip was actually having a pretty good time in Samaria preaching the word of God along with his co-laborer John. Then we discover in verse 26 that there's a sudden interruption. God says to Phillip stop what you're doing and "Go south to the road—the desert road—that goes down from Jerusalem to Gaza." I don't know about you but if I was Phillip, the first thing that would have probably have come to mind is "wait a minute Lord but I'm flowing well here in Samaria, I mean people are being healed and set free and all and quite honestly I'm kind of even enjoying myself, but now you want me to go to Gaza. On top of that you want me to go through the desert! Don't you know that people die of thirst in that place? C'mon God, that wasn't in the plan!" But again, that's just me.

Phillip, on the other hand, kindly went along with no complaints (for that I greatly admire him). As a result of this obedience, we see in verse 27, God set him in the same path of an Ethiopian "eunuch, an important official in charge of all the treasury of the Kandake (which means "queen of the Ethiopians")." To make a long story short Phillip then was able to minister to this young man and ultimately lead him into the faith. But again, the awesomeness doesn't stop there. As a result of this one man's conversion, an entire nation was then able to be introduced to the gospel of Jesus Christ. What would have happened if Phillip decided not to go along with this detour nor allow his schedule to be interrupted? Again, not only would he have a missed out on a sovereign opportunity of empowerment but, as such, so would have an entire nation.

To further drive this point home, there is one more story I would like to share but this one doesn't come from the Bible. It was found off of an online discussion group entitled board of wisdom. The author is unknown but the story goes like this:

## Removing the Obstacle in Our Path

In ancient times, a King had a boulder placed on a roadway. Then he hid himself and watched to see if anyone would remove the huge rock. Some of the king's wealthiest merchants and courtiers came by and simply walked around it. Many loudly blamed the King for not keeping the roads clear, but none did anything about getting the stone out of the way.

Then a peasant came along carrying a load of vegetables. Upon approaching the boulder, the peasant laid down his burden and tried to move the stone to the side of the road. After much pushing and straining, he finally succeeded. After the peasant picked up his load of vegetables, he noticed a purse lying in the road where the boulder had been. The purse contained many gold coins and a note from the King indicating that the gold was for the person who removed the boulder from the roadway. The peasant learned what many of us never understand! Every obstacle presents an opportunity to improve our condition.

Again, I pose the question...what would have happened if the peasant did nothing about this situation? What if like everyone else he simply walked by the problem? Not only would that big boulder have remained there blocking the path of others to come after him, but more importantly he would have missed out on the blessing in store for him as a result of responding appropriately to this obstacle. The same can be said for many of us. You never know when the next obstacle or detour you face has been specifically designed to bring you out on the other side of your destiny. You never know the blessing that could be potentially waiting for you when you choose to conquer your hurdles instead of allowing them to conquer you.

Yes, life may have a way of taking us off guard at times. However, it doesn't mean we have to fall down and play victim to it. Instead, we must learn how to fight for our future, fight for our purpose, and fight for our destiny for truly the victory is not given to the swift or the strong but to the one who is willing to endure. Whether we like it or not, life is a drag down, knock out battle and it's the last man standing who wins. So if you haven't already, make the choice to get in the ring today and stay there. I look forward to seeing you on the other side of your victory!

### Reflection Point

Here are a couple of inspirational quotes that you may want to keep as encouragement while moving forth on your journey...Enjoy!

God knows our situation; He will not judge us as if we had no difficulties to overcome. What matters is the sincerity and perseverance of our will to overcome them. We all want progress, but if you're on the wrong road, progress means doing an about-turn and walking back to the right road; in that case, the man who turns back soonest is the most progressive.

"What saves a man is to take a step. Then another step." – C.S. Lewis

"To get through the hardest journey we need to take only one step at a time, but we must keep on stepping." –Chinese Proverb

MAKE IT A POINT TODAY THAT NO MATTER WHAT, YOU WILL KEEP ON STEPPING!

Made in the USA
Middletown, DE
21 May 2023

31087649R00076